From Thunder to Breakfast

Happy reading!
Gene K. Garrison

From Thunder to Breakfast

Hube Yates and
Gene K. Garrison

Copyright © 2002 by Hubert A. Yates and Gene K. Garrison.

Library of Congress Number:		2001117047
ISBN #:	Hardcover	1-4010-0376-1
	Softcover	1-4010-0377-X

All rights reserved. No part of this book may be reproduced or transmitted in any form or by any means, electronic or mechanical, including photocopying, recording, or by any information storage and retrieval system, without permission in writing from the copyright owner.

This book was printed in the United States of America.

To order additional copies of this book, contact:
Xlibris Corporation
1-888-795-4274
www.Xlibris.com
Orders@Xlibris.com

Contents

FOREWORD
By Hugh Downs 11
Chapter 1
Pioneering 13
Chapter 2
You Can't Go Back 38
Chapter 3
Crisis At The Drive-In Buggy-Wash 40
Chapter 4
Runaway 46
Chapter 5
Prohibition In Phoenix 51
Chapter 6
The Big Bicycle Race 53
Chapter 7
"Where're You Headed, Bub?" 57
Chapter 8
The Fightin' Game 66
Chapter 9
Patsy 72
Chapter 10
Defender Of The Underdog 77
Chapter 11
Attorney Hattie Mosier 79
Chapter 12
The Frog Stunt 82

Chapter 13
I Met Will Rogers 87
Chapter 14
A Day Off 90
Chapter 15
Christmas Projects 105
Chapter 16
A Washtub Full Of Trouble 114
Chapter 17
Peculiar Characters 120
Chapter 18
Fire-Fightin' Preacher 128
Chapter 19
Cigarette-Rollin' 130
Chapter 20
Midwifery 132
Chapter 21
Kids And Animals 138
Chapter 22
The Potato Grenade 141
Chapter 23
A Turtle-Tip 143
Chapter 24
The Old Goat 146
Chapter 25
I Missed You Last Year 151
Chapter 26
Play The Game 154
Chapter 27
The Short-Cut 160
Chapter 28
Crashity-Bang-Boom-Bang 167
Chapter 29
This Is Retirement? 174

Chapter 30
Tinkle, Tinkle, Big Old Elk *180*
Chapter 31
Maybe you CAN Miss It *184*
Chapter 32
The Last Deep-Sea-Fishin' Trip *189*
Chapter 33
The Thirteenth Trail Ride *196*
Chapter 34
The Coddled Egg *202*
Chapter 35
Thoughts on Huntin' *207*
Chapter 36
Skunks and Friends *209*
Chapter 37
Pack-Trips and Weddings *216*
Chapter 38
I Alibied *219*
Chapter 39
I Don't Know How To Be Sick *221*
Chapter 40
The Fall of '76 .... *226*
Chapter 41
The Strangest Wedding *229*
Chapter 42
The Preacher Went A-Huntin' *233*

THIS BOOK IS DEDICATED TO MY WIFE, PATSY.

FOREWORD

By Hugh Downs

Hube Yates was not among the surprises I expected when I moved to Arizona. I had certain sets of ideas about what I could encounter on taking up residence here. I knew there were rugged individualists and reliable, honest men embodying old-time virtues now somewhat eroded in other parts of the country. Hube is all of these, but this is not all of Hube.

When you first meet him you can see he is rugged. You would judge him to be dependable in a pinch, because he looks like he must know the land; and a look in his eye steers you to the notion he is probably pleasant to be around. You might conclude that he is the strong silent type.

On this you would be exactly fifty percent right. He is no weakling. But "silent" is not an adjective that easily adheres to Hube Yates. To our considerable good fortune he has no reticence to loquate.

Two powerful factors make his loquaciousnes a virtue rather than a vice:

(1) Everything I've heard him talk about is worth listening to.

(2) Every subject or event that intersects his life, every experience he files in his almost computer-like memory is stamped with the grace of an outlook that is humane and helpful, devoid of self-centeredness or bitterness, and amused by most of the cosmic panorama.

These are the attributes of large-souled people and if the shoe fits, knowing Hube, I doubt he'll trade one of his boots for it. On top of all this he can be as funny as any narrator I've listened to.

Nobody can analyze someone else's humor, (or for that matter, any humor, since analysis seems lethal to the funniness); and I would not try to tell you why Hube Yates is able to relate the simplest event with uncontrived humor that is simultaneously so subtle and so powerfully funny that you are in danger of falling off your horse if you are on a horse, or rolling into the campfire if you are seated around one, or falling out of bed if you are reading this book where I do most of my reading.

But he is able to do this and, if you are able to read, you are in for a treat in this collaboration with Gene Garrison of some of Hube Yates' life.

Chapter 1

Pioneering

It was 1914—the year that I was eleven—that my minister father moved our family by covered wagon from Guthrie, Oklahoma to Phoenix, Arizona.

As far as the Yates family was concerned, Phoenix was over on the islands. Nobody knew anything about the distance from Guthrie. The only thing we knew about Arizona was from reading wild-west stories.

My father sold the farm to outfit us for the trip West. The farm was a 160-acre claim that he homesteaded when the Cherokee Strip was run.

Dad took the wagons down to the blacksmith shop, had the rims double-bolted and set, and had straps put on. We fixed places to carry water barrels on the sides and the platforms of the wagons. It was quite a chore to get ready to go, especially for somebody who was guessing and listening to stories.

Just after school was out we left Guthrie in two covered wagons pulled by mules. Two pack horses trailed along. We took what trunks and things we had to have because we weren't goin' to come back. We even padded our little organ and took it along.

There were six other youngsters besides me—my oldest brother, Amos, 19; my oldest sister, Ruth Anna, 17; Evalena Pearl, 15; Joe, 13; Esther May, 9; and my kid brother Elmer Leon, 5. I nicknamed him Skeet. My father and mother, James E. Yates and Lilly May Yates, were in charge of this pioneer family.

It was such an excursion to begin with. I wanted to walk miles and miles those first few days. There was always something to do—chase grasshoppers or cottontails. The horses were just walkin' along. We boys looked something like a group of Huckleberry Finns. The girls were dressed in long dresses and bonnets like our mother wore.

We traveled six days a week. On a Sunday, regardless of the campsite, we always stopped and rested the horses and had a church service. We'd unload the trunk-sized organ, which one of us had to pump while Mother or Evalena would play it. During the service my father would open up with a word of prayer, then he would read the scripture, we'd sing hymns and close with a prayer.

It was a nightly proposition for all of us to gather and kneel around the propped-up wagon tongue and say a prayer—nine prayers each evening.

There was singin' other times too. Mother had a good voice. She could harmonize with anybody. I could be way off huntin' rabbits and I could hear where camp was when she and Evalena were singin'.

It took a great deal of nerve, or faith, for my father to take his family and head out into an unknown land. We couldn't step over to the telephone and call an officer of the law when something went haywire. And there was no drug store to stop into for a cherry Coke, and no grocery store when we ran out of supplies. Everything had to be figured out as near as it could possibly be done. Mother and Dad had to count the people who were goin' to eat, count the mules and horses, and figure out what was needed, and what the limited space in the wagons would be used for.

Mother was a little bit of a woman. She hardly ever raised her voice. She didn't have to because the members of our family did what they were expected to—even little old Skeet, who was a manly little boy.

Mother sure had a system to her work. If she had to go across the camp for something, and if there was anything that had to be carried over within the next five or ten minutes, she'd take it so she didn't have to go back. She never started off someplace and then snapped her fingers and turned around to go back to get somethin' else. How in the world a little woman like her could put out so much work for the nine of us, I never will understand.

On this trip some of the meals were postponed. We were hungry together. It was feast or famine. We got short of water many times. When you have all those people and animals drinkin' it, it didn't last long, and our stock got awfully dry a few times. Any time a big old strong mule gets down on his knees and just goes along suckin' the ground, you know blamed well that that mule is dry. He sees mirages, I think, like people do.

We not only ran short of food and water on the way West, but we also ran short of money, which is a common thing in our family.

* * * *

We were gettin' into a different sort of country. Every day or two we'd see a little ranch. We got to a wooded place where there was a little creek runnin' through, with quite a bit of timber windin' across the face of the land. We stopped and pulled over for lunch. My father said, "We'd better unhook and let the horses have the advantage of this green grass."

I started lookin' down this little creek. If there was anything to explore, we always did it. I come up over a little knoll and there was an old shack settin' over there about a quarter of a mile. It looked like it was deserted, so I just walked around among the trees and I came up on a wobbly colt. He was walkin' on something in the sand. I looked down and here his mother was bogged down in the quicksand. The little colt was walkin' back and forth over her back and, from the manure of the colt, he must have been there a long day anyway.

The old mare had fought and fought to get out. She was absolutely all in and was just gradually goin' out of sight. The colt was strong enough to wobble around and nudge the mare's face, but not heavy enough to sink in.

I ran back to the camp and broadcast my findings.

My father and my two older brothers got the rope and went back there. We put logs out for us to stand on. We dug around and underneath this mare and put ropes under her so she wouldn't go down any farther. When we'd take a bucket of quicksand out, the hole would fill with water. It was like a vacuum. You just had to put a tension on and hold the tension and work around her. We finally got her out and washed her off. The little colt didn't lose any time gettin' its lunch.

We decided to go over to the old shack to see if anybody was around. We found an elderly fellow there. He said he'd been ridin' lookin' for this mare and that it was a racehorse. It had been bred to a very valuable stallion and the owner had put her out to foal. It belonged to the rancher that this old fellow worked for. He never thought about the quicksand. When he heard that we got her out of the quicksand he asked, "Is she alive?"

"Yes," my dad said, "so is the colt."

"She's got a colt?"

"Yes. It looks like it's a couple of days old."

The old man brought her up and fed her some hay.

We stayed down on the creek that night.

The man we talked to told the rancher that some people comin' through with a wagon train had saved his horse. The owner was very concerned about that mare. He wanted to hug everybody. He came down to our camp and asked, "Who found the mare?"

My dad said, "My son over there," and he pointed to me.

The man pulled out thirty-five dollars. That was like givin' me a farm in Texas. I said, "I didn't do that for the money," but he insisted that I take it, so I gave it to my mother.

I didn't know, until then, that we were broke. Five dollars would go a long way. Two dollars would go a long way. Thirty-five dollars was a bonanza!

* * * *

Farther west we came upon some burned-out ranches. The first one we came to couldn't have been burned very many days before we got there. There wasn't a soul there. Couldn't have been an accident because there was too much distance between the burned buildings; the fires had to be purposely set.

We were standin' there lookin' at the destruction when a great big old spotted sow come gruntin' and runnin' to us. It must have weighed two hundred pounds and was real tame. It was so happy to see us.

We watered our horses and stayed there overnight.

The sow would eat grass and come right back to us. The grain in the shed was all toasted and roasted, but that pig ate the stuff. Then it'd just lay around our camp.

We started off the next day and that silly thing started off just like we did, followin' us right down a trail.

My father got a stick and we all tried to drive the pig back. He said, "I don't want to hurt it, but it's got to go back. It's got water and feed there and it should stay there until somebody finds that the place has burned down."

Anybody else but my father would have butchered it. Oh, no. My father said, "That pig doesn't belong to us."

We had the blamdest time tryin' to get that thing to go back. Just when we thought we had abused it and spanked it enough and thought we could outrun it, there it would be, right back with us.

Along about noon everything was goin' good. We'd been ridin' for two or three hours and hadn't seen the sow for quite a while. We stopped and heard an *oink, oink, oink.*

We youngsters said, "Why don't we take it with us?"

Dad said, "Oh, it's too heavy and it doesn't belong to us." We couldn't take it with us because he thought that would be stealing.

Finally that plague-take-it pig got so tired that it couldn't follow us any more.

A couple of days before we reached the Rio Grande in New Mexico there was lots of desert and mountains. It was just the way the Lord had made it.

We saw dust way off to the north. We knew it was made and not just a whirlwind or dust devil, and it kept gettin' closer and closer. Then we could see objects comin' into view as they went down through the little draws and canyons. When they got closer we could see a long string of riders—about fifteen or them.

We had traveled days and saw nothin' or nobody. Here we were out in the great big open world and here come a group of riders.

As they got closer it didn't take too much eyesight to see that they were naked except for little clouts about twelve inches by twelve inches. They were hung from their waists with little buckskin thongs. They weren't much protection, actually. This was just like a patch over a man's eye, only a little larger. They never worried about them stayin' in place too much. There wasn't anything in the back.

I don't know what tribe it was. To a little kid in 1914 Indians were Indians. The thrills and the chills were the same, regardless of who they were. We remembered the burned ranch houses and barns we had seen along the way, and remembered the stories of Indian rampages that we had heard.

When they got close to us they looked gold-colored in the sun. One of them had on a brand new stove-pipe hat that didn't belong in that part of the country any more than a grand piano. Another one had on a brand-new pair of black pants, and still another had a brand-new black coat on, one a pair of black slippers, one a white shirt, and one wore a vest. That's all they had on besides their clouts.

Where did they get those things? We noted this with a lot of concern.

Contrary to motion pictures with warring Indian parties, they never made any noise. They never whooped or hollered. They just rode up and stopped about a hundred yards away and looked at us for a minute or two. The man who was apparently in charge said something to them. They didn't point with their fingers. They puckered up their lips and pointed them over here or over there. Then they rode in a circle around our two covered wagons and pack horses.

We were all huggin' the guns we had. I don't think the Indians had more than four guns and they all looked like single shots. They had bows and arrows and had us outnumbered all to thunder. There was only nine of us, countin' the women too. I'll never forget I was huggin' the same gun I used at night when I guarded camp. I had to take my turn even at the age of eleven.

We had good horses and good mules—those big Missouri mules—so I had to help guard them. The gun I had was a 32-caliber. It was made by the Derringer outfit and it was what they called the four-barrel Derringer. When you cocked it, instead of turning a cylinder, you turned the whole six-inch barrel. It was fairly accurate. I could shoot cottontails with it, when we had money enough to buy the shells.

I figured on four Indians if I didn't get discombobulated somewhere. As those fellows stood there my father walked out to the one who was wearin' the cocky stove-pipe hat.

There was fuzz up and down the backs of everybody in our outfit.

The Indians looked down at my father like they were lookin' at an ant. There wasn't one word spoken. My father just walked back and leaned up against the wheel of the wagon. My brother was watchin' from the other side of the wagon. The women had been told to stay out of sight.

Whether the Indians sat there for fifteen minutes or thirty minutes, I couldn't say, but it seemed like hours and hours. It was just that we were so tense and on the fryin' pan that it seemed like a long time, but it wasn't. It was probably thirty minutes that we stared at each other, but it was a long thirty minutes. It was a silence that was almost noisy.

Somebody was on the verge of gettin' shot. Any time anybody is afraid as much as I was, all you've got to do is to make a false move and they'll shoot. A lot of things went through my mind. Whether they figured out that there wasn't enough there to take the chance of some of them gettin' killed, I don't know.

Then, just out of nowhere, the fellow who was in charge said something we couldn't understand, and he pointed south with his pursed lips. They made a complete circle and rode off. We watched them leave just like we watched them come, only with a lot more relief.

* * * *

We finally got out where the land was blamed-near rolly. Sometimes for a mile or so there were little old flats and mesquite thickets.

We came up onto an old dilapidated ranch house. We knew they had water because there were a couple of shade trees there. There were eighteen or twenty horses in the corral in the back that were good-lookin' horses, only they looked kind of drawn.

We were within a couple hundred yards of the house when a man looked up and saw us. He looked like he had been stabbed with an icicle. He turned and hurried into the house. We saw one guy look from behind a window, another one through another window. There was four or five men there—white men. They were alerted when we came up there.

We stopped about a hundred and fifty feet away from the house. My father stepped down off the wagon and walked up to them and asked, "What's the chance of gettin' water here?"

There was silence for a little while. Well, it was a dead giveaway that they were outlaws.

"Sure. Right ahead of you. Uh, where are ya goin'?"

"Phoenix, Arizona."

"Phoenix, Arizona?"

Then they wanted to know where we'd come from. Dad told them and said, "We want to fill up our kegs and go on a few miles farther."

The fellow said, "Well, there's lots of water right there. You'll find feed for your horses about eight miles down. You'll come to a little place down on the wash."

We could see that he wanted us to go on, so we did. We finished the day out. There were no hills, canyons or gullies. It was flat. We must have made nine miles before we camped for the night.

The next mornin' we had the fire goin' good and way off to the west we saw a lot of dust. Sure enough, there must have been twenty riders comin' towards us. They were some of the saltiest lookin' characters I ever saw.

As they got closer we could see the sun shinin' on their stars. It was the sheriff's posse. They were all wearin' six-guns and carryin' thirty-thirties. It was a rough-lookin' bunch.

When they saw us they winged out. They didn't all want to be in one bunch in case there was some shootin'.

The Sheriff questioned my father. "How long you been here?"

"Since last night."

"You didn't happen to see four or five fellows with about twenty head of horses, did you?"

"Why, yes."

"You did?" Then they all squeezed in. "Where did you see them?"

Boy, were they tickled. They'd been trackin' them, but hadn't caught up with them yet.

Dad told them about the house they were in.

"That's Jim's old place," one of the men said. "Thanks a lot, fellow. They stole all those horses. They're racehorses. When we catch up with them, we'll bring nothin' back but the horses."

Boy, how they took out of there, just ridin' for leather.

I wouldn't have wanted to be on the other end. They didn't fool with horse thieves in those days. There was no trial. If there was no place to hang someone they caught, they just poked a hole in their middle. Sometimes they'd take time to bury them, and sometimes they wouldn't.

* * * *

It was so long ago that I can't remember what little old jerk-water town it was, but it was a little old place fifty or a hundred miles from nowhere. There was a general store that sold such things as tobacco, salt, pepper, flour, nails, saddles and harnesses.

The Indians at this little town were just at the point of decidin' where they wanted to go—whether they wanted to be left alone or wanted to go stay on the reservation. There'd be burnin' and plunderin' of the ranches in these out-of-the-way places. It was dangerous.

When the ranchers would have to drive to the general store for supplies, if they lived twenty or thirty miles away, they'd stay in town overnight. They'd have to come down to the edge of a river and go across a big flat. If it was rainy weather, they'd get stuck there and they wouldn't get through.

The Indians got wise to that and directed the water around to this old Gumbo Flat. They'd hang around and work like a dog for hours helpin' people across. Maybe they'd get ten cents or a package of *Bull Durham* or something.

When we come up to that thing it wasn't rainy season at all, but you could see that they had worked like Trojans to get that water to run through there and gum up the detail. It was maybe a hundred yards across. It looked like it was impossible to get a wagon through.

The Indians were all standin' around waitin' for us to ask them to help us snake the wagons through all this loblolly.

We got the horses way around where the mules could see them. We put all the ropes we could on the ring in the tongue of the rig and turned those big old mules loose. They brayed and started off. It looked like we were goin' to lose the mules and everything. The mules would follow the horses through fire.

About twenty-five or thirty angry Indians were standin' there watchin' us pull those two wagons through there. It took a lot of engineering and hard work. By the time we got through, the day was done.

Pretty near everybody who passed would just hobble his horses there and make camp. The grass was good and so was the water. We were weary and hadn't gone anyplace. We hadn't made three miles that day. It was a chore.

The Indians weren't pleasant. The atmosphere felt like it was ready to blow up. It was as frightenin' as it could be.

My dad said, "Let's get the organ out." He had often said, "Music has the power to charm the savage breast." I never forgot that.

We got the organ set up and my sister went to playin' it. Nine-tenths of her music was hymns. My mother's and sister's singin' could make shivers go up and down your back.

You could just gradually feel the atmosphere changin'. We could see the Indians begin to relax. Finally they were layin' over in the brush just listenin' to the music. That went on for two or three hours. Then my father said, "I think we can button up the organ and go to bed. Everything's goin' to be all right."

It was.

* * * *

We began to see the trees and the foliage and knew we were gettin' near water. On the banks of the Rio Grande there were adobe and rock houses which belonged to the Indians. It was a pueblo settlement.

We had to find a place to ford the river. We found one that had been used some, probably by the cavalry.

We crossed and stopped on the west side of the river overnight. We didn't want to stay on the east side because of the Indians. Our recent experience made us a little leery. We pulled off down into a little cove and hid down in there. That was kind of a touch-and-go camp. We were very particular about guardin' and seein' what all was goin' on. We breathed a sigh of relief when we pulled out of there the next mornin'.

We got into Socorro, New Mexico the second day after that. It was a wide place on the Rio Grande. There were people there who could speak English, and, I'll tell you, that was a treat.

We had a horse get sick there from the alkali water. An old horse that's used to the alkali is not affected by it because he's grown up with it all his life, but our horse couldn't take it. We had to stay camped on the Rio Grande for a whole week. We picked up the horse three times a day. We tied a lasso rope around him, and the whole family had to stand him up, and hold him for a while. If he laid down very long, he'd be dead. Horses can't lay down for a long time like a cow. If you don't get them up, they never get up. We had a vet-blacksmith treat him.

In a week's time the horse was standin' up one mornin' when we got up. That was a happy day.

We had been travelin' for two months or more and we wanted to move along to Phoenix—wherever that was.

* * * *

We finally got to the White Mountains in Arizona, just a few days drive west of Springervillle. I was takin' the watch from midnight on. I was alert because my horses were restless. All of a sudden the horses reared up and snorted. I knew that there was a scent there that they didn't know, and I was scared to death.

I saw something about seventy-five yards away comin' toward the horses. The breeze was blowin' from the horses right over him. I was just ready to shoot this guy, when he raised up and I saw that it was a bear. Boy, that didn't help my blood pressure out one little bit. I didn't know that if I'd just hollered at him, he'd break a leg gettin' away.

The horses were snortin' and spookin'. If the wind had been the other way we'd still be huntin' horses. They'd have left the country.

The bear departed for parts unknown. He didn't stay with me, for which I was happy.

When my father came out early in the mornin' to get the horses it was still dark. There, among the pines, I told him about the bear.

He said, "I expect he was more afraid of you than you were of him."

I said, "That's what *you* think."

Walkin' through the pines on the way to get the horses, we saw something else move, but I couldn't figure out what it was. My father said, "What in tarnation is that thing?" "Tarnation" was my father's cuss word.

It looked like a little man two or two-and-a-half feet tall. He'd bounce around from one real dark shadow to where you could see it, and then go back in the shadow again.

My father said, "Let me have that rope you've got." He made a loop, and finally threw it. He was good with it. It landed around this figure that looked like a man.

Just as soon as it settled down, we knew what it was. Holy smoke, he'd roped a civet cat. I'd never seen one before, but I have since.

My father took the rope off as soon as we caught him.

Since the spotted cat had spooked the horses so bad, we decided we'd better get the scent off of it. We took it to the creek and washed it and washed it. You couldn't walk up to a horse with that rope to save your soul. A tame horse would snort and rare back. We dragged it all day and at night we'd bury it in the ground, hopin' the scent would soak into it. We wore that rope out by draggin' it for days and days, but we never were able to use it. The horses would not stand for that cat smell.

The whole night was a spooky night for me. I welcomed the dawn.

* * * *

When we came across the country we had to use our ingenuity in crossing rivers. The first time that we came to one of the Western rivers, we were tryin' to find a place that we could ford.

I looked at the river and saw big boulders just floatin' and bobbin' along like corks. Some of them looked like they'd weigh five or six hundred pounds. It was brand-new to me. I thought, "Holy smoke, what kind of a country is this?"

Every time we forded one of those rivers we had to be sure that the trunks and suitcases we were carryin' were up on blocks so that the water wouldn't get to them. We forgot that one time, and we had to stop and take everything out and let it dry in the sun. Everything in the bed of the wagon was soaked. That taught us a lesson.

There was one mesa that was rough and rocky and hardly had any trail at all. We found a little place that was almost straight down, or so it seemed to me. It was so steep that you absolutely could not put a wagon over it.

My father got the ax out and chopped down two big trees. He chained them on the back of the wagon so they would drag, and chained the wheels of the wagon so they wouldn't turn.

The only way he could get those big old Missouri mules to go was to ride down first with the horses. If a horse goes, a mule will just bray and go through fire to get to them, just like a colt for his mother.

We would point those wagons with the chained wheels down off of those mountains and go right off. The neck-yokes would be stickin' up. The wagon tongue would stick way out and the poor old mules would be just scootin' on their fannies, diggin' holes and slidin' rocks, goin' straight down. The collars were way up on the mules' ears. The trees would dig in to keep us from goin' too fast. They dug rocks out too, so we had little rock slides goin' down with us.

When we got to the bottom of the thing, maybe we'd have several days of good drivin' along the flats.

Sometimes we could see where the Indians had planted corn, but didn't see their villages at all. They didn't have to live right there with it. Nobody was goin' to come and steal it.

When we had to ford a river, we had to go out in it and feel it out. We had to be sure there was no quicksand to lose our horses or mules in, and to find a good place to get across without losin' all of our equipment. Then we'd go down the river until we found a big dry log or two. If they were real dry and there was a lot of buoyancy to them, we'd bring them and tie them on the downstream side of our wagon wheels. We'd get those mules all ready to go and we'd take the horses across. Then the mules would be crazy to go. We put lasso ropes on the wagons and we'd get upstream from them to hold them. We tried to stay where the horses would hit bottom now and then. Sometimes they'd plunge. That's where the treacherous water was.

We'd do lots of driftin' and floatin'. That was quite a dangerous proposition. I've seen such things in the movies and I've seen how wrong they do it. That's why a lot of those wagons roll over and they lose a lot of them. The stage is set for the movies. There are lots of rescue workers right there to help them. Our closest rescue team, I suppose, was on the ninth cloud. There was nobody there to help us.

We forded one river after another like that and on two or three occasions it was really touch-and-go.

* * * *

We were on a big mountain the first or second night out of Springerville.

We had an old single-shot 12-gauge shotgun and had two shells left. We had tried to use one of them time and time again, but it wouldn't go off. We didn't waste them. We couldn't afford to.

My father put the good shell in when we saw a jackrabbit. He said to us, "I'll go over and get that thing."

He was gone longer than we thought he ought to be. We waited and waited, but we never heard him shoot.

Finally one of the kids said, "Look, there he is."

We looked out among the pines and there our father was, runnin' from tree to tree, tryin' to out-manipulate a plague-take-it bull elk. We'd never seen one before. The animal must have weighed over a thousand pounds.

Dad kept the pine trees between him and the elk.

That old bull elk stood with his head sideways lookin' at my father. Dad would run behind another tree and the elk would charge after him. It's amazin' where they can go even with a big old rack on their heads. He wanted to hook something, but Dad finally made it safely back to where we were campin'.

He said, "I didn't want to shoot him. We couldn't handle that much meat." My father just hated to kill things.

We finally used the good shell and had nothin' left but the one shell that wouldn't go off.

When we got around Rice, Arizona, it was pretty slim pickin's with the food supply. One of those big old rabbits would have fit in the pot just right.

My older brother was elected as a committee of one to give that shell one more try. He pulled a bead on a jackrabbit, and it scared him pretty near to death because the gun went off and killed the rabbit.

Of all the times that thing wouldn't go off, it did just when we needed it the most.

We had been livin' on barley soup. I loved that. It was dark colored and had its own whang to it. It gave us lots of strength. We had been havin' that for days, but the rabbit that night added a little variety to our supper. It was quite a treat to get a few mouthfuls of meat.

* * * *

We came in through the old Apache Trail to the Roosevelt Dam. It had been about three years since they had dedicated it, but they were still workin' around there.

We pulled in right down on the river below the dam where there are some hot springs. The water was so hot that I couldn't get in, but my mother could. We got a chance to take all the hot baths we wanted, and you can bet that we needed them. Mother also put out some wash.

The horses and mules were ankle-deep in grass. It was sure a red-letter camp for them.

My brother Joe was a good one to get in a river or stream and catch fish with his hands. He waded out into the river and looked for the fish. He walked back out near the dam where some leftover building equipment was and got himself about a half-inch piece of pipe that was five or six feet long. He waded into the river.

My oldest brother, Amos, said, "Look at him. He's goin' to kill fish with a pipe."

One of the Yates' family covered wagons as they crossed Roosevelt Dam on the way to Phoenix in 1914.
 (Courtesy of Evalina Yates Sills)

While we were standin' there laughin', Joe was standin' in the river where it was only about eight or nine inches deep and KA-ZOOIE! He beat something in the water.

We looked and saw this great big old fish floatin' belly up. It must have weighed six or seven pounds. Joe grabbed it up and carried it over the bank. He threw it down and went back again. Then we all went out fishin', the little and the big.

It was a Saturday afternoon, as I recall, and we stayed all day Sunday to give the horses a rest, to have our church service and to catch those fish. We caught over a hundred. We were cookin' them every way we could think of.

We left there early in the mornin' and went to Tortilla Flats. It was a hard days goin' because the trail was straight up and straight down.

We didn't know what to do with those fish. We didn't want to lose that food, so we decided to dry them. We cleaned them, got some wire ropes and we ran it through their gills and hung them from one mesquite tree to another to dry them.

We had some big ones. For the most part they were carp.

We got up the next mornin' and, talk about somebody lettin' the wind out of your sails, there was nothin' left on those wires and ropes but the fishheads.

There were tracks all around. They looked like little deer tracks, but we couldn't figure what deer would be doin' eatin' fish.

Later we found out that it was javalina that had swiped our fish. That was our first experience with wild pigs, and it left us with a few feelings that are hard to put into words.

* * * *

Three-and-a-half months after we started our trek westward we got into Phoenix and drove up the old Salt Canal at 12th Street and Polk. There was just a little house here and there. It was pretty open.

We camped by the canal because it was a place to water the horses and there were shade trees and lots of grass. It was also close to Garfield School.

My father had corresponded with some people in Phoenix by the name of Sturgis, so he walked uptown and saw them. They came out in a buggy and visited us by the canal. I'll bet we were a sight to see. We probably looked like a bunch of Okies comin' in.

There was no church for my father. He had to organize one. They finally built it at 10th Street and Moreland.

We moved our wagons up in back of Garfield School on 14th Street and stayed there two or three months. Then we got a house at 414 north 12th Street. It was a big brown house—the first one that was built in that block. It was just across the canal from where we stopped first.

When we moved into the house I didn't know whether I liked it or not. I had been outside so long that I felt fenced in. There were four bedrooms, I think, and a big screened porch. I used to go out and sleep in the yard a lot.

This was all brand new to us, but it didn't take very long to find new friends. Kids would come over to ride horses and swim and fish. The boys all got to playin' marbles and spinnin' tops. But we all had our chores to do too.

I even had a cow that I kept at 16th Street and Fillmore. Between 14th Street and 16th Street for four blocks there was a fenced mesquite thicket. It cost me fifty cents a month to keep my cow there. I sold milk to the neighbors.

Our arrival in Phoenix wasn't the excitin' end of an adventure. It was a beginnin'—a beginnin' of one dad-gummed experience after another.

Chapter 2

You Can't Go Back

In 1918 we went back to Guthrie, Oklahoma for a visit. This trip we went by automobile. What a chore that was!

We had a great big old high-wheeled Overland car. Sometimes we'd have eight or ten flat tires a day. We'd pump them up so hard they'd just about pop. We thought we were supposed to pump them until they were solid. We were just abouncin' across the country on those hard tires.

My father didn't know the first thing about repairin' an automobile, but he had to learn. Occasionally we'd break an axle. We'd catch a ride with the first buggy or car to come along. It was such an experience goin' across the country in a car that people would stop and visit with us. "How many weeks you been on the road?" they'd ask.

They'd take us to some town and worry with us until we got it fixed. All us car-owners were joshin' around in the same sack. We were all discussin' what happened to us and what happened to them, and when we found other people in trouble we'd help them out. Those were the pioneerin' days of the automobile.

We were really lookin' forward to seein' the old homestead. In our minds' eye we could see the house, the lane and the barn, the green of the foliage. As we chugged along, gettin' closer and closer, we thought of Dad ridin' a big old buckin' horse down the lane. We remembered the tightrope between the windmill and the barn—and the trapezes. It didn't seem odd to us that our preacher-farmer Dad was as good a trapeze artist and acrobat as most circus performers. He had all kinds of contraptions. He'd get up on the high wire or get to swingin' on his trapeze away up into the peak of the barn. He never even thought to take the farm equipment out from under him. He didn't use a net. He'd swing as hard as he could swing. Then when he'd get all through, he'd pretend like he was fallin'. His feet would catch the trapeze ropes and he'd be aswingin' by his feet.

They never had any celebration in that part of the country at all, but that they'd go get Jim Yates. He'd walk on a tight wire or loose wire or anything. On a loose wire, with the wind blowin' like the dickens, saggin' and awavin', he'd walk out there, do his stunts, lay down on it, and get up. He'd always go out wearin' a pair of bib overalls. Then when he'd get out there and almost fall off, he'd take the overalls off and he had on his tights.

He never got any money for his performances. If he received any, he'd give it to a group of women raisin' money for a charity. He was asked to come to the circus, but he thought he was supposed to go preach.

Those were the memories of Dad on the homestead. We were lookin' forward to seein' the farmhouse and land where we had worked and played, but what we saw was somethin' else. As we drove up to the lane it looked like some demon had tried his best to disfigure the land. Oil derricks were growin' all over the place like wild onions. It was quite a letdown for a kid.

Chapter 3

Crisis At The Drive-In Buggy-Wash

When I was a youngster I decided I'd carry newspapers. We lived just a little ways from *The Arizona Republican*. The old printing press was on Second Avenue and Adams in Phoenix, so it was no trick for me to pick up my papers.

I started out with a city route where they had paved sidewalks now and then, and a little paved street here and there. The out-of-town routes they called horse routes.

Every time it would sprinkle you couldn't ride a bicycle on the adobe streets. Where it was packed, you'd just as soon try to ride across ice as ride a bicycle on it. And if you got where it wasn't packed, it would gum up in your wheels just like glue.

Then when we moved out to the west side of town at 15th Avenue and Fillmore I got a horse route. I'd stop off at the Palo Alto Stables after school and clean stalls and do anything else they wanted done.

As you walked through the place, there was a little cubbyhole of an office. The wagons and buggies for rent were on the left, the tack room and wash room on the right, and straight ahead would be the water trough. They had rings in the posts where you tie your horse. There was a wash-rack for buggies and surreys, with a sump in the middle of it. There were brushes, buckets, sponges and water hoses there. People would come in and get their buggy washed just like they go to a car-wash today. Then there must have been twenty stalls on the right and left. Behind that was where they came down the alley and unloaded the hay. They had a little grainery there, but the horses were overworked and underfed. That's the way a lot of people did in order to make a dollar.

The fellow who ran the place was named Jeff England. He was a real nice old gentleman with a big handlebar moustache, little blue eyes, and he was as white-headed as he could be. He knew horses inside and out. He tended to his own business and he'd squawk at the boys when they'd do things wrong. He talked through his nose, like he had an adenoid problem, so he was hard to understand.

One day a guy come ridin' in the front. He said to Jeff England, "Do you board horses here?"

Jeff said, "Yeh, uh do."

The rider got down off his horse. It was a dandy. It seemed like the horse had been pretty well ridden. He was dusty and lather-stained. The fellow, in his early twenties, looked like he weighed about two hundred pounds. He wasn't fat, just big, black-headed and had black eyebrows. He wasn't a bad-lookin' guy, but I didn't like the expression of his mouth or eyes.

He started tellin' what he wanted done with his horse. He beat the dust off of his hat, looked around, and as he turned I saw he was wearin' a big old forty-five, tied down. It wasn't an uncommon thing to wear a six-shooter. I didn't think much about it, only that it was tied down like he might have been in a hurry.

He wanted his horse in the last stall clear back on the north side. He saw where the grain was, and I recall he gave some to his horse. He didn't want the boys to fool with it at all. He wanted to take care of it himself. He snapped orders around there day in and day out, week in and week out. He was mean.

About the third week he got to be a fixture. They called him Dick. He was throwin' his weight around and swaggerin' around town. He was pushin' the kids around. Nobody could do anything to please him. The kids were all afraid of him. We didn't like to go there when he was there, but as long as he paid his money, old Jeff didn't contest him.

One day I was ready to help Jeff with some of his work before the other kids got there, and another man came ridin' in. He was a stranger to me, and I knew pretty near everybody in Phoenix. This guy would make you look back at him. There was something a little different about him. He was an older man than Dick by about fifteen to eighteen years. He was all silver around the ears. He had only two or three days' whiskers on his face. He was strong-lookin', probably an inch taller than Dick. He had gray-blue eyes, as clear as crystal. He looked like he had gone through the worst dust-storm in the world. He also looked like the kind of guy you'd like to have on your side if you had any trouble.

He asked if he could board his horse there. Jeff told him he could, and showed him which stall to use.

The cowpoke put his horse in the stall, got a gunny-sack and rubbed him a bit and fed him. He never wasted a word on anything.

After he got through workin' on his horse, he put the bar down and started out toward the office. I saw him glance over his shoulder. He turned right straight around and walked back and looked at Dick's horse. He walked around to the other side and looked at him again. Then he walked to the office and asked Jeff, "Who owns the horse in the back?"

Jeff said, "Oh, at balongs to Dick." He told him his last name.

"How long's he been here?"

"Uh, two or tree weeks."

"Where is he?"

"Aroun' town. He'll be in probly abou' four o'cwock."

The fellow thanked him and walked out. I felt that he was no friend of Dick's.

Later I was sittin' up in one of the buggies about even with the water troughs, waitin' for a ranch friend to come in town.

I didn't say anything when the kids came in. They walked right by me and didn't see me sittin' there.

Pretty soon here come old loud-mouthed Dick. He started givin' orders to the kids. He always had to be bullyin' somebody.

About ten minutes later I saw the other cowpoke come in through the front door. He got up within twenty-five or thirty feet of Dick before Dick even noticed him.

The man called Dick by name. Dick never even turned to look at him. He just stood there. The cowboy spoke to him real low. I don't know what he said until he said, "You can turn around, Dick, any time you're ready because I haven't followed you all these weeks for nothin'. I want to go back and tell her where I found you, and where I left you."

That's one time I saw a great big bully beg. The other man insulted and abused him. Any man who will take that is a coward. He said, "What a brave man you are with a woman, and what a cowardly so-and-so you are with a man. Pull that gun and throw it in that water trough. I don't care how fast you draw, I'll just take a chance that you're goin' to throw it in the water trough."

There was something said about comin' all the way across New Mexico, so he probably was from Texas.

He egged him and insulted him. Then he said, "I'm not goin' to quit right there. At least put your hands up and fight."

He wouldn't, so he said, "You asked for it," and he slammed that guy down across the side of the head. The scalp just laid wide open and bled like a stuck hog. That cowardly outfit never offered to defend himself. There was no fight in him.

I was all eyes and ears, watchin' this.

When he finally got through, he said, "I'll tell you one thing, you'll always look different. You won't be the handsome whelp that you were."

It looked like he had chopped him with a meat ax.

He had one more thing to say: "I want to tell you this. I'm goin' to go home and I'll tell her what I did to you. I'm not goin' to look for you anymore, but pray that our paths will never cross again. I won't even speak to you. I'll kill you right where I see you."

He put his foot on Dick's shoulder and pushed him right back down on the wooden floor, went back to his horse, asked Jeff what he owed him, paid him, and rode out.

Chapter 4

Runaway

I guess every kid in his life gets a spasm when he wants to run away from home. The better they treat you, the worse the kids think they're bein' treated.

In 1919 my folks decided they were goin' back to a place just east of Kansas City to a town called Sedalia for a little bit, where they were goin' to put me in school. I wasn't doin' too good in school. I'd been playin' too much hookey. I always left my horse tied to the mesquite thicket outside of Adams School. If I didn't like the way school was goin', I'd just ease out of the window and make a run for it, get my horse and go for a ride, sometimes for a couple of days.

My folks were havin' problems with me and I was just brainless when it come to listenin' to them. I used to like to go down to the stockyards and hire out to those guys who were movin' cattle there on 15th Avenue and the railroad track. I got what I thought in those days was good money.

I was too cocky. I had too many irons in the fire. I had three horses and two burros. You could find me pretty near any time up in the hills someplace.

I had a long, tall, disconnected, skinny buddy named Eddy, who was just as rattlebrained as I was. All he wanted to do was ride and rope. We never did very good ridin' broncs, but he'd come out of the chute on them. He was always gettin' jammed up. I was sixteen and he was seventeen.

He and I talked it over and decided that if my folks were goin' to sell my horses and my burros and take me to Sedalia, the thing for me to do was to run away from home. I couldn't stand to see my horses sold and go back there to school and walk those brick streets with no horses, no nothin'.

I got all packed and primed and we headed west one night. We rode to the Agua Fria River before daylight.

We slept a lot the next day. I shot a cottontail and we ate it. I had about fifty pounds of bran that I had thrown on the pack. That was all the grain we had for the horses. I built up sort of like a tortilla made with water and the bran. I had an old piece of tin that I had resurrected along the road and slid the tortillas on it to bake them. It was real tasty when we were hungry. Between that and the rabbit that I shot, why we got by pretty good.

We stayed by the Agua Fria for a couple or three days and decided we'd go up on the SH Mountains out of Buckeye, where we'd been before. There were a lot of wild horses up there. We decided (big dreams, you know) we were going to go out there and rope those wild horses and sell them.

We were both pretty well-mounted, all right, but I don't think his horse could have caught one of them. It wasn't that rugged a horse, but it was beautiful. My horse was a hard-lookin' outfit. It was a Navajo color and was roped wild up in the Graham Mountains. I had worked on a ranch for a couple of years to buy the horse. It was salty. It'd just run all over those wild horses.

We must have spent two or three days on the dry river-bottom where nobody could see us. Then we headed towards Buckeye. I think we had twenty-six cents between us when we got into town.

We bought something to eat and decided to go back to the canal where there was lots of green grass. There was a world of feed there for the horses, so we hobbled them in the beautiful grass.

We went on the canal bank and piled our clothes on top of each other and went for a swim. We were plenty dirty.

We were havin' a big time when we heard *bumpety, bump,* and saw the dust of some old car comin' so we peeked up over the bank. My heart stood still. I hadn't heard tell of anybody lookin' for us or anything.

My dad drove right up, stopped, walked over to the camp, looked around and didn't see us, picked up my six-shooter and stuck it in his belt. There wasn't anything for us to do but get out and put our pants and boots on.

He hadn't seen me for about four or five days. He didn't ask me if I was comin' home or anything. He was too smart for that. He said, "We'll go down and see if we can board those horses and pasture them for a while."

He took our pack and stuff and down we went. He told this guy we had to have pasture for our horses.

"Oh, sure," he said. "How long will you need it?"

"A couple of months anyway," Dad said.

We left them there and I finished another month of school. All this time I wasn't doin' any ridin' at all. As soon as school was out I went to work in a harvest field. All around the valley where these homes are settin' now used to be grain fields and small ranches.

I worked for about a month and got the money to go to Buckeye to pay my pasture bill.

Eddy wasn't workin' with me, but his folks gave him some money.

I got off on a Saturday afternoon late. We got some fellow to take us down to Buckeye in an old T-Model Ford. Holly smoke, what a rough ride. I decided it was all right to go without a saddle, but this buddy of mine had his.

We went down there and asked the fellow what the damage was for the horses. He told us. It was very reasonable.

We caught the horses and, say, they were so full of thunder that I had to borrow my friend's saddle and break my horse over again. He just bucked and bawled. I got the smoke all out of him and gave Eddie his saddle back. His horse didn't buck. Mine had been caught wild and he was just a little bit that way.

It was about a forty-mile ride back home. I'll tell you, that was quite a chore. I didn't feel like ridin' him very much the next day either.

By runnin' away, I escaped goin' to Sedalia that year, but they got me the followin' year. My parents made me sell my horses and go back to finish my schoolin'. That wasn't too good an idea either, because their schoolin' back there was far behind ours in Arizona. It was pitiful.

Chapter 5

Prohibition In Phoenix

One midnight in 1919 was the end of buyin' drinks legally. Prohibition had passed. You can imagine what the old miners, cowboys and hangers-around had to do before midnight. They tried to drink it all up. They carried bottles away from the Palace Saloon and hid them because the next day there would be a federal law prohibiting the sale of alcoholic beverages.

The Palace Saloon was on the northeast corner of First Street and Washington in Phoenix. That's where nine-tenths of all the business transactions were made. Rather than have deals made in a lawyer's office, people would go in the saloon, make a deal and shake hands over a bucket of beer. Millions of dollars worth of business was transacted that way.

Phoenix at that time boasted of two sprinkler-wagons. They were pulled by four horses and they'd go down the dirt streets, sprinklin' them with water. They'd sprinkle all the outlyin' streets around town between 7th Street and 7th Avenue, and between Roosevelt Street and the railroad tracks.

On the first day of prohibition the sprinkler-wagons were driven up beside the saloon to collect the alcoholic drinks that didn't get consumed the night before.

Men started wheelin' that stuff out—gin, wine, whiskey, champagne—everything. They'd pour the liquid into the sprinkler-wagons and throw the empty bottles into another wagon. When they got them filled up, the drivers of the water-wagons started out right down Washington Street sprinklin' the streets all the way to the Capitol buildin'.

I was only sixteen at the time, and I stared at the spectacle. I'll tell you, guys that had been tryin' to drink up all the booze all night were followin' the sprinkler-wagons, tryin' to catch the liquid in their hats. They were slippin' and slidin' around. Saddle horses and buggies and people on foot followed the wagons.

The drunks would collect maybe half a hatfull and stand in the street and try to drink. Maybe they'd get two or three swallows. Some of those guys followed that thing until they fell down. People just laughed at them.

Soon after that, ceilings in the houses around town began to sag. They were pot-bellied and cracked. People had stored case after case up in the attics of their houses. Houses then in Phoenix were just built for shade.

Prohibition had a peculiar effect on people. People who had never taken a drink would say, "Who's goin' to tell me I can't drink?" They'd start drinkin' that old rot-gut stuff and go *blind* and go crazy and everything else. It made a lot of alcoholics out of people who never drank before.

Chapter 6

The Big Bicycle Race

On May 1, 1920, when I was workin' for Chambers Transfer Company, I took the day off to be in a bicycle race from Tucson to Phoenix. I was seventeen at the time. My kid brother, Skeet, drove us down in a Model-T Ford.

Before the race I had gone down and got me a little silk sign lettered *CHAMBERS TRANSFER COMPANY* and had sewn it on my jersey. I got me a visor to wear on my head and cut me a cardboard bill about ten inches long and attached it to the visor. It was real light. I had put on a big heavy sweatshirt and I had a pair of rasslin' trunks—big, wool rasslin' trunks. People looked at me, and no wonder. I'd get that outfit wet like a sack around a canteen. It stayed cool for hours.

The mornin' of the race a fellow at work had asked, "Where's Hube?"

"He went to Tucson."

"What've we got goin' to Tucson?"

"He entered that long-distance bicycle race."

"From Tucson to Phoenix?"

"Yeah."

"Who went with him?"

"Nobody."

Holy smoke, he blew his stack. "Somebody take that new Dodge pickup. Here, take some money out of the cash register and see what kind of help he needs. You sent him there by himself?"

Meanwhile, down in Tucson, there were twenty-six of us lined up ready to start. In those days there was no haven between Tucson and Phoenix. We had to go by way of Florence before this other highway was put in. It was a hundred-and-forty-four-mile ride.

Someone fired a gun to start the race. The other racers started ridin' like they were goin' only a quarter of a mile. They just went into it as hard as they could go. I counted them as they went by. I think there were six or seven that passed me.

We got to the edge of town and started toward Florence, which is half way. When you got out in that desert, you could just take the road you wanted. Wagons had been haulin' wood across it, makin' trails everywhere. The dust was like powered sugar. As your pedals would come over, they'd go down in it four or five inches. You'd just wobble and stagger around from one ridge to another.

We got through those mountains out of Tucson and then the roads got pretty crooked and gravelly. They were easy to skid off of. I passed by one fellow, then another. Finally I saw one guy who was settin' his pace a little faster. He came around the corner pretty fast and went off down the canyon. When I came by I looked over and he was draggin' up what was left of his bicycle, but he was all right. That left three fellows ahead of me. I set my pace a little faster.

I could hear them talkin'. "I don't know who that guy is behind us there. He's ridin' our fannies off. This hot desert will slow him down."

Pretty soon I was gettin' a little closer. It was before we got to that old windmill that sets about halfway to Florence, about forty miles or so out of Tucson. As I recall, I rode up to these three fellows and one of them said, "Hello, uh, Yates. Why don't we stop at this windmill and get some water?"

It was hotter than a firecracker. I said, "Oh, I'll get a drink in Phoenix."

I kept on goin' and that's the last time I saw them until I was in Florence. We all had to stop there for an hour and be checked by a doctor. Forty-two or so minutes after I'd arrived, here come two of them in.

But before I got to Florence, the fellow in the truck met me just outside of town. He asked me what he could do for me. I told him to go in the drugstore and buy some little bottles that would hold about two big swallows of water. "Fill them full of water, throw a wet sack over them, and don't make me stop to get a drink. Ride up aside of me when you can and hand me one of those bottles and I'll just wash my mouth out and drink what I want. It'll save me stoppin'."

He said, "Any time you want to get in here and throw a kiss at this race, climb in."

The driver described it after we got back. "I watched his legs," he said, "watched them 'til I liked to went crazy. Hot . . ." Oh, his profanity was enlightening. "I watched for hours and hours and the farther he got, the faster he went."

There were only three of us that finished out of the twenty-six. I was an hour and forty-seven minutes ahead of the next one. My time averaged a little better than seventeen miles an hour.

There was no pavement at all until I got to Tempe, east of Phoenix, and then there was only a little bit. I had to cross the bridge over the Salt River and then go up over that mountain to get into Phoenix. Now it's cut straight through. Then the only pavement we had in Phoenix started at 16th Street and Van Buren.

The problem the other racers had was that they were dehydrated out there. I wasn't. I looked like I was dressed for the North Pole. They came and asked me about that afterwards. I explained that you could put a sack around a canteen and it will stay cold a long, long while. Then maybe you'll have to wet it again. Those guys just baked in the sun. The silly thing they did was to go out in that boilin' hot sun with not enough on to flag a handcar. Some of them lost their minds. Someone had to go get them and take them to the hospital.

My prize for winnin' was a new suit of clothes, a medal with all the data on it, a new Elgin watch, and a lovin' cup. When it was written up in the paper they called me Leather-Lungs Yates.

Oh, yes—my kid brother, with all those ruts he had to go through in the Model-T, arrived back in Phoenix several hours after I did.

Chapter 7

"Where're You Headed, Bub?"

When I was only about eighteen years old I used to go up to Colorado with my family and work on some of those cattle ranches with my friends. It was just a way of spendin' the summer.

I got to likin' a girl over in Bayfield. I always managed to get there the Fourth of July so I could show off in front of her and ride some of those buckin' broncos out of the chute.

I got real close to her. I mean we thought we were in love anyway. I used to leave Phoenix each year when my family would go up into Colorado. I'd always go up and see this girl—red-headed and cute as a bug's ear.

We had been there most of the summer and it was gettin' near school-time. My kid brother, Skeet, and my kid sister, Esther, had to go back to Phoenix to start school.

Rather than put them on a train that took a roundabout route, my father decided that I should take the T-Model Ford and drive them straight through to Gallup, New Mexico and put them on the train there. That went straight through the pie. We could do it faster and cheaper. Then I'd turn around and go back up to Colorado and bring my mother and father to Phoenix maybe a month later.

We packed up all of their stuff and started out. There were just the three of us and my big old fightin' bulldog, Sam, who looked like he was doctored up for the movies with his one black eye. He had a head twice as big as he ought to have. If somebody had a dog that wanted to fight, why it wouldn't take long to discourage them. I used to be pretty proud of him.

Comin' off the Wolf Creek Pass down at the bottom on the south side was what they call Pagosa Springs. The mountain had switchback after switchback.

We were comin' down off of this Wolf Creek Pass battin' along. I kept feelin' my brake-bands. You'd just run in high gear and away you'd go. Everything had to be braked. You had to keep hittin' them and hittin' them. I'd use my reverse because you didn't use reverse much anyway. There were three pedals—low, reverse and the brake. You fed the gas with a lever up by the steerin' wheel.

I wore out so many of those T-Model Fords. A fellow gets so after a while he can feel what he can pull and what he can't pull with them.

I kept afeelin' my brake to see if it was gettin' hot. I finally decided it was, and I shoved it down in low. I tried my reverse. I tried them all. The first thing I knew, I didn't have anything. I was goin' about thirty miles an hour around one of those bends and there was no way to stop.

I could see way off to our right—the bottom of this canyon and the river. We were travelin' like the dickens. I didn't say nothin' to anybody. I didn't have time to say anything. I kept watchin' for a place to dump the car over.

Finally I hollered back to Skeet to roll down to the bottom of the seat, and I reached over and grabbed Esther around the shoulder and pulled her down under the steerin' wheel where she'd be protected. I just laid that car upside-down right in the middle of the road, all four wheels in the air. The luggage and everything else we were carryin' went from thunder to breakfast all over the road.

Nobody was hurt. We got out but I didn't have any bulldog. I said, "Where in the thunder is he?"

We looked to a kink in the road, a switchback about three-quarters of a mile or better, and saw him runnin' away from us just as hard as he could run. I called and called and yelled and yelled. My voice was echoin' through the canyon.

Finally he stopped in the middle of the road, way down. He had run a couple of miles, but he was down on the mountain, below us. He barked and barked like he had seen something spooky in the sky. Then he turned around and started runnin' back toward us.

The three of us dumped that silly Ford back over on its wheels, pushed it off the road and put some rocks in front of the tires so it wouldn't roll away. I relined the brakes. I always carried an extra set of brake-bands and oil. In those days you carried oil as much as you carried water. I had two or three gallons of oil, five gallons of water, lots of patchin' material, a pump, tools, and a jack.

We went on to Bayfield that night.

This girlfriend's family and ours were pretty close together. Skeet and Esther knew them all.

I told my girl's family I was goin' to make this run to Gallup and I'd leave early in the mornin'. I was goin' to go through Farmington, across the San Juan River and go through a hundred and four miles of Shiprock Desert.

Today it's all black-topped and you can travel that just like nothin'. It used to take about a day-and-a-half to make it. It was just like drivin' in plowed ground. Cars today couldn't go over that road any more than they could fly. It was something.

I said, "I'll try my best to make it back day after tomorrow. Then I won't have to be back up to where my family is for a couple of days and I can stay and visit my girlfriend."

Her mother was all fired up over it. She said, "That'd be wonderful!"

We went across that Shiprock Desert and I found the train for my brother and sister to take. We only had a couple of hours to wait. We got the tickets, got everything organized and I saw them off.

Then I went to the gas station to fill up. The fellow there said, "Where are you headed with all this equipment? You're not headed for Arizona?"

I said, "No, I'm goin' north."

Just kind of soft like a prayer he said, "North? Across the desert?"

"Yeah."

"When you goin'?"

"Tonight. Just as soon as I get this thing filled up."

"You're goin' across the Shiprock Desert at night?"

I said, "I just came over it today."

"Yeah, but what in the world do you want to go back for?" He swore like a Trojan.

I couldn't understand his reaction. "I'm not afraid of the dark. What's wrong with tonight?"

He said, "You haven't been readin' about what's goin' on, have you?"

I said, "No, I just got here. I just came down from Colorado to take my kid brother and kid sister to the train so they can go back to Phoenix to go to school. They've got to enroll next week. I'm goin' back to pick up my mother and father."

He said, "Well, I'll tell you somethin'. You'd better wait and go in the mornin'. You won't meet one car out there in three or four days."

"I know it."

"Yeah, but you know what they've been doin'? They've been robbin' people out there. There are a bunch of thugs nobody's been able to find. It's a hundred and four miles from my service station here to the San Juan River. That's all bad country now. People have been beaten and robbed. Why, I wouldn't go across there tonight for all the tea in China. Who've you got with you?"

"Nobody."

He said, "I won't sleep tonight thinkin' about somebody goin' out there by himself. You're outnumbered. You'd be outmaneuvered. There's just absolutely no sense in that."

I said, "Well, there is when I've got a red-headed girl over in Bayfield that I want to see. If I get over there tonight I can spend a day and a night at her parents' place."

"Oh, man, what a guy won't do for a woman. You're crazy!"

I had a couple of hours before dark, chuggin' along the old Shiprock Desert in low, then in high, with my bulldog, Sam, sittin' beside me.

The road looked like plowed ground. Boy, ridges and ridges. Those old high-wheeled Fords could just crawl over them, *bumpty, bump*. I had to hang on to the wheel with both hands. I was feedin' the gas with my right hand and the spark was on my left. If it was timed a little bit too fast I'd shove it up. Course, in those days you reached down and adjusted your carburetor to fit your elevation. There's no sense in it not bein' that way now either. It would save gas.

I had been drivin' an hour or two after dark. I was someplace in the middle of the desert, chuggin' away in low gear. If I saw a blur up ahead but could not see clearly, I'd shove my clutch in and race my motor so the magneto lights would brighten. Then I'd let my clutch out. It was almost like havin' a lantern.

I saw somethin' flash up in front of me. I was goin' through a big cut in a rock pile. You couldn't pass anybody in there. If you made it yourself, you were lucky. When I raced the motor and the lights went up, all the yellow in the Yates family went up and down my spine. There was a high-wheeled 1914 or 1915 touring car. The driver rode straight across the road and closed the gate on that gap.

I thought, "Well, this is it. I'm goin' to go out like a light. When they come out here to pick up my body they'll have a few other bodies to pick up too. I'm goin' to kill every jackass that walks up to my car." I was scared to death.

I was wearin' one of those big old Army coats. It was too big for me. I slipped my forty-five into my sleeve.

I drove up to the car blockin' the road. It was empty. Sure enough, right out of the dark came a guy. There was a reflection off of that Dodge car from my lights. He came over to the passenger side of my car and leaned in. I can still see the evil smile on his face. He said, very slowly, "Where're you headed, Bub?"

Right then something happened that I never had a dream of. I thought I was there all by myself. I knew I was goin' to feel somethin' on the back of my neck, and he'd tell me to get out. When that guy leaned forward, good old Sam lunged at him, missed his throat and bit him between the neck and shoulder. You think he'd turn him loose? He shook that guy until he looked like his head was goin' to go clear off his neck.

And scream—I've never heard such screamin' in my life. Boy, he was just beggin' and pleadin'.

Well, I was scared. I knew what had to be done. That dog was goin' to kill him, that's all there was to it. That old sixty-five-pound bulldog shook him just like a sock. He liked to have knocked that guy's brains out on the end of the windshield.

Sam was wearin' a harness, not a collar. I reached over to

hold him, but I couldn't, so I just let him go ahead and shake him. I still thought somebody was goin' to shoot me from behind. There were guys there, all right, but they didn't know what was happenin'. They were just as scared. The screams this guy was lettin' out, if he had been a partner of mine, I'd have wondered just what demon had him.

I had this blamed gun in my hand. I stuck the gun-barrel in my dog's mouth and pried it open so the guy could get loose. I said, "You move that car or I'm gonna kill you."

I was all fuzzy up and down the back, scared to death and lookin' around, ready to shoot somebody because I was afraid somebody was goin' to shoot me.

The guy jumped up runnin' and fell down, jumped up and fell down again. Dust was just like powered sugar in those ruts. I could see the blood runnin' all over. He jumped in the car, started it, killed it two or three times. He made three or four attempts and got the thing out. Boy, I stepped on that low gear and ground away through there. My lights were bright. I expected every minute for somebody to shoot me all to pieces.

I went *chug, chug* up the road, got it in high gear and went on out. I was sweatin' like a Trojan.

I looked at Sam and saw part of a blue shirt and an undershirt that he brought along. He got that guy down where he lived.

When I got into San Juan I told a fellow in a gas station about it.

This guy said, "Say, I want to tell that to the Sheriff because there sure have been some terrible things goin' on out there. They rob people of their watches, rings and everything. We'll be keepin' an eye peeled for somebody that's torn up."

I said, "You won't have any trouble. He's tagged on the left side."

And off I went toward Bayfield to see that little red-headed gal. At the time I thought it was worth the night's ride.

Chapter 8

The Fightin' Game

I had a brother two-and-a-half years older than me. He was overbearin', and as strong as a bull. When he couldn't stir up anything, why he'd just bust you and you'd say, "What in the thunder is that for?"

He'd say, "Well, it's a free country, isn't it?"

My stars, he was strong. I told him, "I'll be gettin' a little bit better all the time. I'm still growin'. One of these days I'm gonna clean your plow until there's just not a cow in Texas. I don't care how big you get. I'm gonna whip you if it's the last thing I do."

It went on like that for years.

After a while he got married and went to live in the Midwest. He was back about four years later to visit us at our big old house on East Pierce Street in Phoenix.

What he didn't know was that I had taken up boxin'. I was just afigurin' on guys like him.

He couldn't stand to leave me alone. He had to see if he could whip me.

I said, "You never give up, do you?"

He just kept goin' and kept goin'. I said, "You'll never know until I have to do this, so you'd just as well come on out in the front yard and let's get it over with."

I took him outside and darned near beat him to death. I was talkin' all the time. Oh, he was a bloody mess. I didn't let him hit me.

Dad walked out and stopped us.

I said, "Any time you're not satisfied, brother, nudge me." He didn't pester me any more.

I'm not butchered. I've sparred with some of the champs who've come through Phoenix. When they wanted somebody to work out with them, they'd get me to do it. Some of them got real rough and I knocked them out. I learned something from all of them. I found that some were overrated too.

* * * *

It was said that a fighter called Spider, who was a southpaw, could whip anybody. You always fight a southpaw with your right hand.

I watched him, and thought, "I don't get it. I just don't get it. Why doesn't somebody knock him on his one-spot?" I wanted to work out with him so badly.

Finally I got the chance. We had gone two rounds when his

manager came in and stopped the fight. He was cussin' and yellin', "Get that guy out of there. He makes Spider look like a beginner."

The manager had dark eyes and black eyebrows. One eyebrow was kind of cocked and he squinted one eye. He said, "Spider's not up to himself today."

A sports writer said, "When Hube Yates fights them there's none of them in shape." He thought I could whip anybody my weight in the country.

Spider didn't say nothin' in the ring, but back in the dressin' room he come over and said, "I'll tell you one thing. I don't give a hoot what my manager says, you sure got two good hands, fellow."

Then this fighter, Bob Webb, who was a light-heavy, came over from the coast. He weighed about a hundred and seventy pounds, while I weighed about one-sixty-three at the time.

Bob was tattooed all over. He'd just see how many of his sparring partners he could knock out. If a guy needed a dollar, he'd go in the ring and try his best to knock Bob over. Not many fellows would work out with him.

Someone came and got me. "Bob Webb's in town. He's the guy who's been knocking out all his sparring partners. I thought I'd tell you before you go down there."

In the ring Bob said, "We're just goin' to mess around. I've got to get loosened up a bit."

The sports writer come to me and said, "I heard that tommyrot. He'll knock your head off if he can. Hube, you keep your eye on him."

I went out there to box him and I watched him real carefully. He threw three or four punches at me. Boy, if he'd hit me, I'd been asleep yet. It was like he was killin' snakes. I'd box with him and push him away and box with him again. He was just bull-doggin' me and throwin' punches that anybody ought to throw at a main event to end the fight quickly.

There must have been a hundred people there to see the workout. I didn't have any enemies out there. I never was overbearin' and didn't like anybody that was.

I was puffin' away at the end of the first round and the sports writer was tellin' me, "You know what he's tryin' to do, don't you?"

I said, "Yeah."

"Keep your eye on him this round, for thunder's sake."

I said, "I'm goin' to change my style. I'm goin' to drag my right foot and forget to back up."

I started off just the way I did before—jabbin' him. I got it set up just right. He was followin' me and I was measurin' him with my left hand. I threw that right hand and hit him just a touch high. He went down just like he had been hit with an ax. I looked at him and he was out. He was cut just above the eyebrow. That whole bone was stickin' out.

I went over, crawled through the ropes and went back to the dressin' room to shower.

Oh, what a commotion there was. He was here for the main event and he couldn't fight.

Afterward he said to my boss, "Some sharky down there, he

didn't throw nothin' away, and he watched me all the time. If I threw somethin' away, he plugged the hole up. You should have seen this guy."

My boss laughed about this.

Guys like that were the main reason I wanted to learn to box.

* * * *

I was billed at one time to fight Jack Dempsey. When he staged his comeback after his fight with Gene Tunney, after that long count, there was nothin' Gene could do but give him another go at it.

A fellow by the name of Doyle, who was a promoter, came to get me. He said, "Jack Dempsey is going to fight on his comeback trail. He's going to fight four men four rounds or less. Would you fight him four rounds?"

I said, "Sure." I wanted to do that anyway. I considered Jack a friend of mine.

I was workin' out hard, tryin' to remember everything I'd seen him do. I had to be careful not to be caught in the trap of his left hook. He could cut you in two with it.

A few days later the promoter came bustin' out and said, "Hey, the heavyweight champion of Mexico just contacted me. What a terrific crowd he'll draw. Would you feel too bad if I put him in there in your place?"

I said, "Thunder and blazes, no. No, go ahead."

At the sound of the bell that big bucket of lard walked out

there and Jack threw a punch at him and grazed him and he went down. Why, he spent more time on the floor than he did standin' up. He got through and got his money.

I told Jack afterwards, "He took my place in there, but I'll tell you one thing, I would have made you work for it."

Jack said, "Wasn't that a hell of a note?"

I said, "Yes, it was."

I never got to fight him. Maybe it was a good thing.

Chapter 9

Patsy

When I was about twenty we used to have lots of church activities with the young people at the Church of Christ in Phoenix. We had a group, maybe eight or ten couples. They'd run from sixteen years to probably twenty or twenty-five years. A few of them were young married couples, but most of them were single.

We called ourselves the Upstreamers. I got stuck year after year as president of the thing. I was always takin' them somewhere because I knew the state pretty well. On Friday nights we'd go to Flagstaff or up to Roosevelt Dam, or Stoneman's Lake. We'd get a chaperone and take our food, swimmin' suits and fishin' equipment.

As a rule, we went on a Friday night and came back on Saturday night so we could go to church on Sunday. When we didn't get back for church, I'd hold a service for the group out where we were campin'.

I had been goin' with a girl who was a lot of fun and such a nice girl. I'd been goin' with her for a long time, but I told her, "I'm goin' to quit." Quit goin' with her was what I meant.

She asked, "What did I do?"

I said, "Well, you didn't do anything. But I don't want to get married and the first thing you know, the two of us are goin' to take a back-flip and I'll be with you so much that I'll fall in love with you until I can't see. There's no use to subject you and me both to that because you're human and I am too. I like you and have fun with you, but I don't want to get married, and if I don't quit goin' with you, I'm goin' to fall in love with you, and I want to quit. I don't think anybody ought to play with anybody else's heart-strings. I'm goin' to quit while I can still get away without too much hurt."

She said, "You waited too long to get away as far as I'm concerned."

I said, "Dad-gone it, honey, I've been tellin' you all the time, for thunder's sake, just let's have a lot of fun together, keep our noses clean so we won't fall in love. I'm afraid it's goin' that way, I'm goin' to quit."

She asked, "There's nobody else?"

I said, "There's nobody else."

So for about three weeks we met at parties. We'd hang on to each other like leeches, I guess.

One night the group met at the church before a wienie-roast at Hole-In-The-Rock. We had the lemonade, ice cream, wienies and marshmallows in the car.

I saw two girls come in and I didn't know them, but I thought I had seen one someplace before. I went to my buddy that had double-dated with me and fought on the same fight-card, and barnstormed all over the country with me, and I said to him, "Ed, who is that blue-eyed girl sittin' right over there?"

He looked at her and said, "I don't know. I never saw her before."

It kind of upset me.

We tried to see who-all had rides out and how they were grouped to ride. I asked this blue-eyed girl how she was goin' out.

She said, "I have my own car here, but I don't know anything about the country. I just got here yesterday."

I asked, "From where?"

She said, "Beloit, Wisconsin."

"Oh? You haven't been out here before?"

"No."

"You haven't been to one of these meetings before?"

She said, "No."

I asked, "Do you know me?"

"No, I'm sure I don't."

She came out here with her sister, her grandmother and her auntie—drove in an old Dodge touring car.

I suggested that her sister go with my buddy and I'd ride out with her in the car.

"That'd be wonderful," she said.

I liked the blue of her eyes, she was soft-spoken and I liked everything about her. I couldn't get it out of my head that I didn't know her from someplace, but I really didn't. It didn't seem like she was a stranger at all.

I decided I wanted to get better acquainted, so on the way out there I took her all over the dad-gummed valley. When we came back we came right straight back.

After I had dated her out a few times, she said, "It was kind of odd that it took us so long to get out to the wienie-roast, and we came back so fast."

I said, "Well, I had to get acquainted, that's for sure."

We were both twenty-one when we got married. We tied the knot in Phoenix at our church at 10th Street and Moreland.

Today, as I look back on it, over fifty years later, it was the best day's work that I ever did in my life. She's a jewel. Yessir, my wife is a jewel. You can't appreciate it, hearin' somebody say it. She put up with me and the way I liked to do things—from huntin' camps to fishin' camps, fightin' and every blamed thing. Of course, I got to seein' it her way.

Incidentally, I named my wife Patsy. Her real name was Lois Townsend.

There was already a girl in our group named Lois, so when I found out her name I wouldn't call her Lois. I said, "I'll just call you Patsy."

Her mother and her brothers started callin' her Patsy. Everybody went for that name.

Chapter 10

Defender Of The Underdog

There was always somebody who wanted to throw his weight around. I'd tend to my own business as long as I could, until it got too ragged. I just hate to see a bully wipin' his shoes on some helpless guy that don't want to fight back or can't fight back.

At a firemen's convention in Phoenix, when I worked for the Fire Department, I went to the bar in the Hotel Adams lookin' for a buddy of mine. There were a lot of roughnecks, would-be cattlemen, and bronco-riders there. I found old Bill sittin' on a stool. The little guy wouldn't weigh over a hundred and thirty pounds soakin' wet. He only had one eye. He got one eye knocked out over at Glendale cuttin' wood when he was a kid.

Some great big old cowpoke was havin' words with Bill. He said, "I'm goin' to bust your head off like I'd bust a grape off a vine."

I listened to it a little bit. Then Bill saw me. "Hello, Hube, how about a drink?"

"Yeah, I'll take a ginger ale."

The big guy made light out of that—that I was havin' ginger ale. He started raw-hidin' me. Then he started back on Bill.

Bill and this guy rolled off their stools, ready to go. I tapped this guy on the shoulder and I said to him, "Did he tell you about me?"

He said, "Hell, nobody told me nothin' about you."

I said, "Surprise parties are never any fun."

"What kind of a surprise party?" he asked.

"Why I just signed a contract with him this mornin' until this convention's over."

"What kind of a contract?"

"To do all of his fightin' for the next three days."

It wasn't my fight, but he was too big and strong for Bill. I just put him to sleep right in the middle of the Adams hotel.

It takes more nerve for me to sit and let a guy rawhide me and give me fits and starts over nothin' and I know dad-gummed well I can whip him with either hand than it does for me to get up and knock his can off.

I've been workin' on it. I've kicked over the traces only once—maybe twice. I told my wife I was goin' to be a disciple of peace and harmony, and I have been tryin' ever since. Besides, I know one thing for sure—it's easier on old clothes.

Chapter 11

Attorney Hattie Mosier

One of the great characters of Phoenix was Hattie Mosier. In the 1920's she dared the City of Phoenix to pave the street in front of her Central Avenue house. It was paved except for about two blocks that she owned. It was the roughest two blocks you ever rode on in your life. You couldn't see for dust. A horse would do a split on account of the ruts.

And when they were buildin' the warehouse between Polk and Taylor Streets she tried to discourage the builders. She didn't want them comin' in and buildin' a warehouse beside her home. She would go to the second floor of the buildin' and bump into something so it would fall off on the workers. She'd knock a piece of brick off and it'd land beside some guy. He'd look up and she'd say, "I'm sorry." She harassed them for years and years. Oh, it cost them a pretty penny to build that warehouse. They finally wouldn't let her in their buildin', but she owned the property all around it.

She was an attorney in long skirts. She always looked like somebody threw clothes at her and she just buttoned them up.

Even the kids knew who Hattie Mosier was. I was about twenty-three when I got acquainted with her.

She spent her days fightin' the City of Phoenix. I don't think she was ever married.

"Hube Yates," she said, "my joy in life is to fight these plague-take-it city politicians. A lot of people like to fish, some people like shows and musicals. I studied to be an attorney and I've practiced it for years and years. The greatest fun that I could possibly have is winning a case. Oh, that's better than a vacation."

She was a good attorney—as sharp as a tack. Some of the city administration finally tried to soft-soap her, but she could see through it.

I enjoyed her because of her intestinal fortitude. She could have made a dozen fortunes by practicin' law. She'd say the right thing at the right time the right way. The weight of her ability to put it over was great. Oh, boy, could she nail it down! She'd talk so nice to her opponent. She'd hold him up with one hand and slap the tar out of him with the other.

Discrimination against women was terrible then. Men would beat their desks and say, "Woman's place is in the kitchen." That's all you could get out of anybody.

One day after winning a court case, Hattie accidentally met the opposing lawyer outside of the courthouse. She had tied him up in knots in the courtroom. He was so mad he could hardly see. He was standin' there just frothin', lookin' at her from under his hat brim.

Hattie said, "I thought we got out of the courtroom just a few minutes ago."

"Yes, but let me tell you something," he said. "Dammit, I couldn't say this in the courtroom . . ."

It was warm weather. He took his hat off.

There were some doves up above in the olive trees and one of them let go and it hit him on the bridge of his nose. It ran right down. It couldn't have been timed any better, right when he was fired up to a hundred and seventy and tryin' to tell her off.

"You know, you lost a case," Hattie said, "but you've got lots to be thankful for."

As he was daubin' the mess with his handkerchief, he said, "What have I got to be thankful for?"

She said, "That cows don't fly," and she walked off.

Chapter 12

The Frog Stunt

Years ago down at the Fire Department we had a baseball team. We had a big yen to beat the Police Department's ball club. It was an annual occasion for the policemen and the firemen to go to Riverside Park and have a rip-snortin' time.

I can still see the Chief of Police. I don't know how he ever got on first base. He must have weighed three hundred pounds. They either walked him or he made a hit.

Somebody brought him a little chair to sit on. You couldn't even see the chair when he was on it. It was like he was sittin' on air. Somebody else gave him a little parasol for shade and a cold drink.

We'd go to Riverside park on our off shift and practice for the annual event. We worked out hard in the hot sun.

There was a drinkin' fountain at the north end of the grandstand with a lot of grass and stuff growin' around it. In this grass was a whole bunch of these little old toad-frogs. They're desert toads.

I looked down there while I was drinkin' the water and the Captain of the No. 1 Station called, "Now don't you guys overdo that drinkin'. You've been out in the hot sun too long. Don't load up on that cold water."

I reached down and picked up three frogs and washed them off real quick and held them in my hand. I let some more water run over my lips and some guy yelled, "Hey, you're goin' to get sick."

The whole team gathered around, discussin' the ball game and drinkin' water.

I walked away from the fountain, leaned over and made a special point of havin' the team see that I was gettin' sick. I had sympathy all over the place immediately. I had slipped those three little frogs in my mouth and pretended I was gaggin'. Those toads were kickin' up a storm.

One fellow said, "Just let her go, you'll feel better."

As I pretended I was gaggin' I let one of those little old frogs come out. Another was just kickin' to get out.

There was a hush.

I made a retchin' noise and out came another one. I straightened up and said, "Listen, be careful about drinkin' that water. It's absolutely full of frogs."

Some of the guys like to have heaved up their shoe soles.

The touchiest guy in the Fire Department was one that would get up and leave if you talked about killin' a fly. The sport we had with him with bugs and frogs and little snakes was something.

Somebody said, "Grab those things and come on back to the Fire Station. Frosty Wilson is on duty. We'll drag you in and you'll be awfully sick, and you let those things go."

I said, "Wait a minute. He'd be all over me with sympathy-plus." But I couldn't resist. "All right. I'm appointin' Big Nasty to stand right over him and when I spit these frogs, you latch on to him. As soon as the shock is gone, he'll knock my head off while I'm bent over."

Big Nasty was the nickname we gave to Clint Nafsinger. He wasn't fat—just a big man, a giant.

I got the frogs in my hand and they dragged me into the station. My spikes were clankin' on the cement. They took me right straight to the water fountain. Everybody was sayin', "What's the matter with Hube?"

Somebody answered, "Oh, he drank too much of that water. It was too hot and it just got him."

Here come the Assistant Chief runnin' over and he said, "Too much sun and water, huh?" He put his finger on that ice-cold faucet. He held me and squirted me with water. I had to take it. Then here come old Frosty. I still had the frogs in my hand. Everybody was tellin' him what the trouble was.

He said, "Let it go, partner. We'll mop it up."

I leaned over and put the frogs in my mouth. I let one go and he hopped around and I pinched the next one on both back legs with my lips. He was just akickin'. Finally, I let him and the other one go.

There was a hush over that place that nobody could describe. It was just plumb silence.

Then all of a sudden everything broke loose. I heard old Wilson yell and Big Nasty grabbed him. They finally drug him out and I got away. He had all the rest of the day to cool off.

* * * *

I pulled that frog stunt other times too. One time my buddy and I went to San Luis Valley in Colorado. Instead of a rodeo they have what they call an Annual Stampede. It's a big affair. I mean the town is so full of cowpokes and horse handlers, cow handlers, and feed handlers, as well as sightseers, that you had to just squeeze your way through. It's just a little town.

There's lots of artesian water there. Naturally, there are a lot of little toads there.

I got right in front of this buddy of mine and said, "Ed, I'm goin' to go over by that fellow in the white hat who's sellin' hot-dogs and I'm goin' to pretend like I'm sick. When the cowboys come up I'll tell them not to eat the hot-dogs."

We stood there on the high curb. Ed put his arm around me as I was feignin' a terrible sickness.

The nicest lookin' little old gray-haired woman you ever saw come up to me and said, "What's the matter with the cowboy?"

Ed said that I had eaten a hot-dog that made me sick. Well, the hot-dog man hadn't sold me anything, and he was gettin' a little hot under the collar.

The gray-haired lady glared over at him. She sat down on the curb beside me and wet her handkerchief and washed my face. She was just huggin' and motherin' me to death. Boy, I felt like I was about an inch high. Why hadn't some old cowpoke come and sat down beside me?

All this time I had a mouthful of toads. I finally started gaggin'.

She said, "Let it go, honey. Don't you mind me." She pushed me off of her breast so I could lean over.

There were a whole bunch of people there. "One of the cowboys is sick. Maybe he got hurt today." It was all sympathy.

The toads were gettin' a little dry and short of air. I let those things go and I just didn't have the heart to stay there to elaborate on it at all. I left the whole crowd there watchin' those toads hop.

I felt terrible about that—a little motherly lady old enough to be my grandmother. That's one time that trick made me feel a little bit short. Dad-gum me anyway.

Chapter 13

I Met Will Rogers

I met Will Rogers when he dedicated the Coolidge Dam in 1930 up above Globe, Arizona.

The President of the United States was there. Cal Coolidge was never a public speaker. He probably could have done it with a pen, but he wasn't a speaker. Old Cal stood up there and just barely moved his lips. What he said didn't amount to nothin'.

The next speaker was Will Rogers. He got up there, chewin' gum and spinnin' yarns, and he said, "You know, I got my feelin's hurt. They brought me thousands of miles to speak at this dedication. There I sat." He looked at his watch. "There I sat for fifteen minutes listenin' to him. I timed him. He stood there for fifteen minutes, and he never said a blamed thing."

People, includin' Cal Coolidge, were just dyin' laughin'. Will Rogers was the only man I knew at that time who could slam the first man of the land, and get a hand for it too.

Rogers said, "But you know what? He didn't disappoint anybody, because nobody expected him to say anything."

Then he started talkin' about the dam. "You know what they done? They ought to feel proud of this. Look back up on the hill there." He pointed to tents and tepees. "Those people for generations have lived right on the bottom of where the water is goin' to be. Somebody decided that they needed water here where the Indians planted corn in that fertile soil. So they drowned this town out."

It was true. The Indians were sittin' up among the cactus and brush.

You know what? There are twenty-four or thirty-six people down below here who are goin' to have water all over their place and they'll be able to raise some corn."

He slam-basted the thing. He's the only one who gave us an idea of what in the thunder they'd done.

* * * *

I saw Will another time when I was captain of the Fire Department's Rescue Squad. Our crew went to all the special events. We were there not only in case something blew up, but to prevent it from happenin'. So when Will Rogers came to perform at the Shrine Auditorium in Phoenix, I got acquainted with him backstage.

He was just as common as an old shoe and twice as bright as a polished shoe. He had a mind that worked like a trip-hammer, and he talked with a drawl. His wit just rolled out of him like water out of a spring.

When he came out on the stage, he'd chew gum and do all kinds of curlicues with that little rope. He'd be talkin' and chewin' all the time. He said, "You know, Phoenix is a nice town. It's a peculiar town. It's different. You know what they did? They invited me to join the Country Club." His hair kind of flopped down over one eye. "Yeah, they did. Of course, it's different from other places. I've been invited to donate to 'em in lots of other towns."

He talked about flyin'. He had been flyin' with some hot-shot pilot in England. He said, "We went around and around one of those big towers there. I didn't know they stood for such things. I do lots of flyin'. My recommendation is never to fly with any private individual. If you're goin' to fly, fly with some of the big companies where the planes are inspected and the pilots are tested every so often."

The very thing he told the American people not to do, he did. He went barnstormin' with Wiley Post all over the country. The plane didn't have any wings hardly. That thing had to cough once and it went straight down. That's what killed him. When the plane the two of them were flyin' went down in Alaska in 1935 we lost an ambassador to the whole world.

Chapter 14

A Day Off

When I was the driver for the No. 2 Fire Station on 9th Street and Van Buren in Phoenix, I got to thinkin' how much fun motorcycle ridin' was, so I bought me a big old Harley-Davidson. I hung up my saddle and spurs and for a year or two I tinkered with motorcycles. I got me a sidecar to haul Patsy and Jimmy, the only son I had at the time. If you don't watch your P's and Q's, you'll crack a motorcycle up.

Friday, February 13, 1931 was a day to remember. I took the day off, put my bulldog, Sam, in the sidecar and decided to take a ride up to Cave Creek, Camp Creek and Seven Springs. To come out to that area you had to hang on with both hands. You didn't dare drive over fifteen or twenty miles an hour or you'd be thrown out.

I decided I'd visit my buddy there at the Ashdale Ranger Station. He used to come to the fire station and visit me quite a bit. I stopped to see him, but the station was all locked up.

I backed the motorcycle and sidecar over under a tree and ate the sandwich that I had brought. I hadn't been sittin' there very long until I saw five wild burros come into a corral next to a barn by the ranger station. I sat real still. They were attracted by the rock salt in the corral. They kept inchin' in until all were in the corral.

I sneaked over near the corral and ran and slammed the gate.

There was an outside stair to the barn loft. I went up and found me a rope. I made a lasso and caught one burro and tied it up to the fence. Then I got on it bareback and turned it loose to see how far I could ride it.

I ended up ridin' all five of them. They would head out through the brush, cactus and mesquite, just abuckin' and ascattin'. They'd dive right through a mesquite tree. I rode some of them way down the creek.

After I let them all go, I was just pooped, but I had had my fun.

Before the day was over it started drizzlin' rain. It got pretty cold so I decided I'd better leave.

I put the rope back up in the barn, left the gate open, fired up the motorcycle and started off. It started snowin' about that time and after I had gone about a mile I could hardly see to drive. I had to go real slow because I'd have slid right off in the canyon in that three-wheeled outfit. Pretty soon it started hailin'. It just beat me and my bulldog something fierce.

I had another old jacket in the sidecar, so I put it around Sam and buttoned it up. There he sat like a funny little man with a grumpy expression on his face.

It took me a long time to get back in the valley. It was late in the afternoon, and I had to go to work that night.

I went by the house and left my dog, went down to work and found all the guys standin' around in a big huddle. It looked like they had been waitin' for me.

A guy named Bill always chewed tobacco. He'd get such a mouthful of juice and keep right on talkin'. He'd have to tilt his head back to keep the tobacco juice from runnin' down his chin. He gurgled through the juice, "Hube, it's too bad you weren't here this morning.'

"Why?"

He said that there was an old man marooned on the island above Joint Head Falls and the Sheriff wanted someone to swim out and get him. The river was at flood stage.

Bill told the Sheriff, "Only one damn fool works here, and it's his day off."

While I was out chasin' wild burros and gettin' hailed on, someone from the Sheriff's Department had been down to the Fire Department to borrow my boat. I had a twelve-foot boat—oak and mahogany—that I had had a guy make for me.

Ordinarily the Salt River is dry, but when it floods, it's savage. If you haven't seen the Salt River in a flood, you've missed something. It was about a mile wide. I knew, because I swam across it just for the heck of it about a year before when it was floodin'.

Bill, the fireman with the mouthful of tobacco juice, told the officer that if I'd been there, I would have gone out and got the man who was marooned.

One of them explained, "We wouldn't let any of them have your boat because nobody knew how to handle it. Nobody's got any business out there unless he can swim. Just above the falls there is a little island. If a person couldn't handle a boat real good, he had no business out there."

It was gettin' dark.

The more I thought about it, the more I remembered that there was an old man who had built a shack out of paper and tin and stuff on this island about fifty yards above the falls. He could walk out there when it was dry. He couldn't swim. It was a fellow by the name of Newtson from Chicago. Tuberculosis had sapped his strength. He was really old at sixty-three.

Someone had heard him yellin' in the mornin', and went to the Navy recruitin' station where they were supposed to have a gun that would shoot a rope out. It fizzled out and they couldn't get it to work. They went to a swimmin' instructor at the college at Tempe—Tempe Normal—to get him to swim out and get the man. He said no.

The island had all washed away except one great big cottonwood tree that was so big that two people couldn't reach around it. It was layin' in the rapids, goin' back and forth, the roots still holdin' it.

Bill said, tiltin' his head back, "The old man is probably drowned by now. Stayin' out in this kind of weather, he's dead now."

I said to Lester Barnum, who was my officer, "I'll get Delgado to work for me, and I'll go out there and see if there's anything I can do."

He said, "If you're goin', I'll go with you." He drove me out there in an old Moon car. It looked like we were comin' up to a circus. There were people out there by the hundreds. We had to use our lights. The hail was beatin' down on the cars like somebody was throwin' rocks at us. People with all kinds of things over their heads were standin' around out there in the night in the hail.

Somebody said, "See that out there where the spotlight is? That's a man hangin' on to the limb of a tree and the tree is about to wash over the dam. It keeps goin' back and forth. The water is risin' all the time. There is a report that there is twelve or fourteen feet of water goin' over the dam. If he goes over that, there'll be no need for people to stand out here and wait."

"What are they goin' to do about it?" I asked.

"What can anybody do about it? They've tried everything. The Sheriff's Department's been here and the Police Department. What do you suggest?"

I said, "I suggest that somebody swim out there and . . ."

"Oh, get away from that," he said. "They'd laugh you off the perch."

I got to talkin' to somebody that Lester knew, and he had a great big old rope.

I started sheddin' my clothes. It was dark and people were so close together that I thought nobody could see me anyway. I was standin' there in my pants and about that time somebody hit me on the shoulder and said, "What do you think you're doing?"

I said, "I'm goin' to swim out there to that old man. Why?"

The Sheriff said, "You put your clothes back on or I'll put your fanny in jail. The idea! It's bad enough for that old man to die without some idiot like you goin' out there and dyin' too. Put your clothes on!"

Lester pops up and says, "Well, I want to tell you this: if anybody can swim that river, this man can."

"Oh, you want to go to jail with him?"

I had to put my clothes back on. I was shiverin' like a leaf in a windstorm. I had handed my clothes to some guy that I knew. I went up the bank and forced myself through the crowd.

I got up there and saw a rope layin' on the bank. I undressed again and handed my clothes to my friends, took the rope and stepped off into the ice-water. It was still hailin'. The air was so cold that the water felt kind of warm.

About eight or nine feet out, that current picked me up. Bridge timbers from the new bridge they were buildin' up above came tearin' by. Even a drowned horse went by. The current just banged me down there about a hundred feet and slammed me into the gravel bank against the trees. I couldn't carry that big old rope.

And who did I see when I crawled out? The Sheriff!

"Well, you satisfied now?"

I said, "Pretty well."

Oh, did he chew me out. I went back and started to put my clothes on. The Sheriff followed me. Nobody could see me if he'd leave his light off of me.

I'd told a fellow that the rope was too big to work. I said we needed a window-sash cord. I knew then that you had to have both hands and both feet to swim those rapids.

A guy from Tempe said he had a whole skein of window-sash cord.

I said, "Lay it on the bank and just feed it to me as I can take it."

I undressed again. I tied a knot in the cord, put the end of it between my teeth, and put the rest of it over my shoulder. I eased off into the river.

I swam to about five or six feet above the old man. When I came down to him I didn't have the slightest idea of what to do with him. I just didn't want him to die out there with nobody tryin'.

He was above the water from his armpits up. If he'd been down in the water he wouldn't have been so cold.

The spotlights on the bank looked like stars shinin' through the hail. I don't know what the people on the bank could see.

I reached down and picked the man up. I was out there at least an hour and the only thing he said to me was, "You did make it, didn't you, lad?"

I saw something in the light in the water. It was a little old box he had made to mix mud in to patch his shack. It was about six inches high, probably four-and-a-half feet long, and about two-and-a-half feet wide. He had an old skid chain wired to the front end of it. When his island got under water, he just stepped in this box. Any port in a storm. It supported him a little bit and when the tree went down the chain was hung up in the tree, and there he had stayed all day in water up to his armpits.

When the box started to float away, I just reached over and grabbed it and put him back in the thing. Then I started pullin' the window sash cord. It's a pretty comfortable feelin' when you've got that knotted rope in your hand and it's connected to land.

I started to put half-hitches around this old gentleman, below his arms and around his waist. I wasn't sure he was goin' to get back alive, or me either.

It was so noisy just above those falls that you couldn't hear yourself think, but they were hollerin' at me all the time from the shore. I could hear them screamin' for me to get off.

Well, I wasn't goin' to swim over there and then leave that old man. I just quit listenin' to them. There was more water comin', the crowd yelled. I thought, "What's the difference? You can drown in seven feet of water just as easily as you can drown in twenty-five feet of water."

I tried not to pay too much attention to them. I was loopin' that man in a cocoon of half-hitches. I tied that rope on to the end of this box. I was afraid to turn it loose because I was afraid he would go over the falls. I kept feelin' the knots with my lips in the darkness because it was so cold I could hardly feel anything with my hands.

I yelled and screamed for the man on shore to pull the rope. They pulled it. The old man was about froze and was humped up in this box. He tipped forward like a fishin' plug goin' down to the bottom of the river. Cold shivers ran up my back. I jumped just as hard as I could jump just as they were pullin' him away. I got to that box and grabbed the ropes and pulled back as hard as I could. It rared up and he went out of sight in the darkness, just skippin' like a sea-sled. He took a buggy-ride! I thought, "There he goes. There's nothin' for me to do but go home."

I crossed my fingers and eased out into the river. I finally got to shore and felt the gravel beneath my feet. They couldn't see me comin' out of the river because it was so dark. I'll bet I crawled through three hundred people, stark naked.

I listened to the conversations on my way to the car. "Somebody said somebody swam over there."

"Naw. Hell, that's a joke."

I got over to this blamed old Moon car. When you opened it the lights went on. I was in a thunder of a fix. I just fell in. The only thing I had in there was my undershirt. Where were those guys who were still draggin' my pants and shirt? It was noisy in there because of the hail. Lights began to come on. Here I am tryin' to huddle up in there and cover myself with my undershirt.

I yelled, "For thunder's sake, will you please turn the blamed lights off of me." It was not a question. It was an order.

People opened the car door. I threatened them and slammed the door, and then they'd open the other side. I was freezin'.

Then a woman crawled in with me. She was kind of whimpering. She said, "I just want to ask you a question."

Well, there I sat with this undershirt in my hand.

She wanted to know if I made it over to the man.

I said, "Yes, mam. I did."

She asked, "There was no way in the world to get him back, was there?"

"Yes, mam. He was back before I was. He's probably in the hospital by now."

She just screamed and cried. It was her father.

* * * *

About a year-and-a-half after the Salt River incident, I was gettin' ready to go on a deer hunt at the Kaibab Forest in northern Arizona. I was twenty-five minutes behind schedule already. I was at the fire station waitin' for the mornin' shift to come on, when a taxi drove up. A man got out, came in, and said hello to me. Then he said, "Do you know Hube Yates?"

I said, "Yeah, I sure do. I hope you haven't got any truck with him."

"Does he work here?"

I said, "Yeah." I had no idea who this well-dressed stranger was.

"Know very much about him?"

"Yes, I think I know more about him than anybody. If he owes you some money, does he know anything about it?"

"Oh, no. He doesn't owe me any money."

I was sittin' there wonderin' who the heck would be so interested in me. He kept askin' questions and I threw a curved ball to everything he said. He wrote it all down.

I said, "If he owes you any money, you're in a thunder of a fix. Talk about hard pay, boy, you have to squeeze him to get it."

"What kind of a guy is he, anyway?"

"Oh, my, I don't want to use that kind of language this early in the mornin'."

We were goin' on like that, and then he said, "You know, it's a funny thing. I don't have any idea how many people I've talked to in the past ten days, and you're the first one who gave him a black eye."

I said, "Wait a minute. Why do you want to know about this Hube Yates anyway?"

"I'm his attorney."

"Oh, no. I know you're out of gear. What the thunder does he need an attorney for?"

"Well," he said, "I don't know whether you know about Andrew Carnegie, but I'm an attorney from the Carnegie Hero Fund Commission."

I asked, "What has this Carnegie got to do with Hube Yates?"

"You surely know enough about him to know about the swim he made out here in the river to save that old man's life."

"Yes. I do recall that."

He was still writin' as we talked. "We'd better start all over," I said.

He said, "What do you mean—start all over?"

"Well, I'm Hube Yates."

"You're Hube Yates—the fellow who made that swim?"

"Yep."

He wadded up the notes he had made and put them in his pocket. Then he asked me a different type of question: "Were you afraid?"

"Who wouldn't be afraid? You haven't got time to stop to worry about it. You're afraid after it's all over, and you get to thinkin' about it."

He asked, "Can you take me out to that place?"

"I can go with you in a few minutes."

"Let me see where it was, take some pictures and measure it."

When we got there he said, "My gosh, this is the falls that they were talking about."

There was only about four or five feet of water goin' over it at the time.

He asked me some more questions and thanked me. That was the last I heard about it for a while.

Then one mornin' I was listenin' to the news at the fire station when the newscaster said, "Here's one you Phoenicians would like to hear. There's not a handful of you in Phoenix who don't know this guy." He started talkin' about ball-playin' and boxin'. It sounded like he was talkin' about me.

Then he said, "It's none other than Hube Yates. We just got word from the Carnegie Hero Fund Commission that he has been awarded one thousand dollars and a Carnegie Hero Medal. They're as rare as hens' teeth."

That was the first time I knew anything about it. The guys looked at me and I looked at them.

Soon the award arrived in the mail. A thousand dollars was a lot of money in those days. It paid off the mortgage on our house.

As far as savin' the old man was concerned, I don't deserve as much credit for it as you would think because it wasn't anything new to me. I know that it takes more guts when you're afraid. I had done dangerous screwball things like that all of my life and I had the breaks. I'd been over falls and rapids. I swam an impossible place for a piece of cake on one 4th of July.

I found that you can do most anything on Friday the thirteenth if you have it pushed on you.

* * * *

One time I was huntin' doves at the Salt River with my cousin Charles. Everybody called him Chicken.

Wearin' Levis, boots and hats, and carryin' rifles, we came up out of the dry river-bottom and saw three people sittin' on higher ground around an old shack.

I kept lookin' at this old man. I thought it was the same old man I had got out of the river two or three years before, but I wasn't sure. You see, I didn't have any time to pick any daisies out on the island or pay much attention to what he looked like, for that matter. The only way I could see him was under the floodlights from over on the bank.

I didn't know whether he would try to rebuild on the river banks or whether his daughter would take him someplace else to live. I didn't have any idea the old gentleman would be back out there any more.

He started lookin' at me and I spoke to him.

It messed up the party. That old guy just went to pieces. The poor old fellow was so happy to see and thank me that he just broke down and cried.

He told me that he got my name from the paper. He had heard that I was a fireman. All he could think about was a fireman for the railroad. He had to walk six miles to Phoenix and went from one place to the other lookin' for me. Now that was twelve miles each trip. He went twice and gave up.

He had one foot in the grave and the other on a banana peelin'. He was just livin', that was all.

His shack was similar to the other one, but was built next to the dry river-bed instead of right in the middle of it.

A week or two later I took Patsy and young Hube by to see Mr. Newtson. Hube was just a little button then.

The old man told Patsy, "If I'd aknown this, that this young man had a family, I'd have turned loose of there and gone over the falls before I'd let him come out there and do that."

Then he said to me, "You treat it lightly. But look, Mr. Yates,

I was out there all day. There were thousands of people there to see me die." He shook his head. "How did you come to do it?"

To me that was a kind of lopsided question because I couldn't understand it.

What are you goin' to tell a guy like that?

Chapter 15

Christmas Projects

I had a buddy I used to hunt with years ago. His name is George Smith, but everybody called him Smitty.

He used to go up on his property out of Williams and cut Christmas trees off his ranch up there. His boys and I would help him. He'd come down to Phoenix and sell them just to make Christmas money. It got to be a thunder of a project.

This was around 1930 or so.

After he got the trees to the Christmas-tree lot, I'd go and visit with him. We'd have a fire and put a piece of elk or deer meat over the coals and have something to eat while we waited for customers.

People would come in to buy the trees, but as a salesman Smitty would have made a good blacksmith. He'd stand there and let the people shake the trees all around, pick them up and paw through them. They could do as they blamed well pleased.

When people would come in I'd get up and go wait on them. Phoenix was much smaller than it is now and I knew many of the people.

Smitty had another load or so of trees that he had to haul down from his ranch, so he suggested that I run the place while he made the trip. I got my bedroll and threw it out there on the Central Avenue lot.

We were real short on Christmas trees when he came back two or three days later. He had cut piñon trees that time. They held their needles for months and months. Those other little old things, people would cut them in the middle of the summer, bundle them up and put them in cold storage. Then at Christmas-time the customers would spread them out in a warm room and you got nothin' but sticks. The needles were all in the carpet. The fresh-cut piñons would take terrible beatings.

I asked, "How did you find out about this?"

He said, "You know, I always run a trap line up there after huntin' season. I just set a trap, put a drag on it, cut a bough off one of these trees and put it on the trail so I'd know where my trap was. Those cut boughs would stay there just as fresh and green until I'd come through in the winter. I thought what a Christmas tree that would make!"

At that time they were sellin' cedars, spruce and fir. Then the people found out about the piñons. They weren't as susceptible to fire as the dry trees.

When he came in with the other load, I had people waitin' for them. I sold the load right off the truck.

Smitty said, "Say, would you want to stay here? We'll go up

and get another load. The boys and I'll work day and night. Let me stay completely away from it. You sell two to my one anyway."

I got rung in that way. I stayed and sold them for him.

When I'd get down to eight or ten trees and didn't want to sit around waitin' for customers I'd set them near the street, put a sign on them and leave a little jar there. When I'd come back I'd have nothin' left but a sign and money—right down to the penny.

People would say, "How do you get by with that?"

I said, "I don't know. I just give people the chance to have the Christmas spirit and be honest about it."

If I had any trees left, I'd give them to the schools and to hospitals.

For ten to twelve days each year we'd make all the way from eight hundred to fifteen hundred dollars just there on that lot. It was a nice deal for Christmas every year.

Another Christmas project was playing Santa Claus for some of the lodges and churches. The lodges had to rent a suit for me. They had to pay a hundred dollars a night for the costume. Then it was outlandish. But they didn't have to rent a beard for me. I had my own. All I had to do was comb this Hollywood whitening in it. It would wash right out.

One children's party was held at the hotel Westward Ho. My goodness, they had so many kids there that I thought the whole world was kids.

My oldest son, Jimmy, was just a little bit of a button. At the party somebody said, "Santa, are you goin' to be back after while?"

I just nodded my head.

Jimmy said, "That's not Santa Claus. That's my daddy."

How in the thunder did he know? He didn't see me in the costume at home.

I went to the mike in the room where they were holdin' the party and talked to the kids a while.

Some little bit of a girl who talked real good was gettin' closer and closer. Finally I motioned for her to come on. I asked, "How'd you like to sit on Santa's lap?" as I picked her up. I kept talkin' to her. Her hands kept gettin' closer and closer to my beard. Finally she got ahold of it, tangled her fingers in it and pulled and pulled. With a voice about a quarter of an inch high she hollered, "Mommie, it is the real Santa Claus. It is! It won't come off!"

People just roared.

After I had a conflab with the kids, we gave away presents, fruit and candy until it was scandalous. My goodness, it looked like tons of it there.

Then I looked at the young woman at the piano and I remembered her. She married an old fishin' partner of mine. She didn't know me from Adam. I said to her, "Florence, why don't you come over and visit with Santa?"

It was like stabbin' her with an icicle. She walked over real slow, and, oh, how she eyed me.

I said, "Florence, sit down here on Santa's knee just once again. You're a grown-up girl now. It seems only yesterday you were like these little tykes, and I used to bring you presents and fill your stockin'."

The crowd was gettin' a thunder of a pick-up out of this. She was flabbergasted.

I said, "Time gets away, but it's real nice to see that you're takin' care of the little ones like we took care of you. You were a nice little girl and I hope you remember to be a nice young woman, like it seems that you are."

She tried to say something, but it wouldn't come out.

I went ahead and put this show on real good.

When I was ready to leave, I had to go down about five doors to a dressin' room. I walked as fast as I could walk. I'd just turned into the room and she came down, hit that door and walked right in.

"No, you don't, Santa Claus, no, you don't. How did you know who I am?"

I said, "I used to bring toys and presents to you when you were a little tyke."

"All right. Sit down once more and talk to me."

I said, "Well, I hate to throw you out of gear like this, honey, but did you ever hear of an old cowpoke called Hube Yates?"

"Oh, Hube!"

* * * *

Then there was a fellow there who ran to my dressin' room and asked, "Are you goin' someplace right now?"

I said, "I'm just goin' to the Christmas-tree lot. There's a gang out there singin' carols. There are some people that are just catchin' up on their annual visitin'. I don't get to see them only when they come up to the ranch." That was the ranch at Heber that I had bought for a huntin' ranch.

He asked, "Could you just give me an hour?"

I said, "I suppose so. What do you need?"

"I've got all the neighborhood kids together at a party. We've got the presents, but we don't have a Santa Claus." This little bit of a fellow said, "You know what kind of a Santa Claus I'd make." He didn't weigh over a hundred and twenty pounds soakin' wet.

I said, "Let me run by the Christmas-tree lot and tell my wife where I'm goin' so she won't worry about me, and then I'll come on out."

We had a big bunch of urchins there when Santa came bustin' in.

"Oh, gosh, oh, gosh," this one little girl kept repeatin'. I got a bang out of that.

* * * *

I played Santa Claus at different churches. It was lots of fun just to look at the sparkle in the kids' eyes.

I went to Camelback Inn to their big Christmas party and played Santa Claus for them. They were nice parties, but I liked it a whole lot better in the little churches around town.

* * * *

Then there's the outdoor Christmas Pageant which Cave Creek has put on since the early fifties.

One year after we moved there the pageant organizers came to me and said, "Do you have any idea where we can get some goats or sheep for the Christmas Pageant?"

I said, "I can get you some sheep, I'm sure, because my neighbor fifteen miles to the west of me has a sheep ranch."

I went over to the ranch and told them what I wanted.

"Hube, I got a pet ewe here that's got twins, and they're as cute as a bug's ear."

Another neighbor had some goats, so I got two goats and a couple of kids. I loaded them in my station wagon, which was a mistake, as we found out later. That station wagon smelled of goats until we got rid of it.

We brought the animals to Cave Creek and put them in a pen. They were just as tame as they could be.

At the pageant they almost stole the show. When Mary and Joseph entered, the baby lambs and kids would play. Then they got down on their knees and just sucked and sucked, with their tails awaggin'. People couldn't take their eyes off them.

As soon as the pageant was over they put them back in

the pen near the pageant grounds, but the blamed goats got out.

We had about a week of roundup. I'll tell you, we'd be lookin' for them all day, and somebody'd call and say, "I saw the goats. They were near such-and-such house."

I'd saddle up and away I'd go. If there was anybody around, they'd go with me. We had one set of wranglers after another. Everybody in the country tried to catch those dad-gummed animals.

I rode my horse almost to the top of Black Mountain. I would have made it clear to the top, I guess, if there hadn't been so much cactus. You can't get through that cactus in places. It's all rocky too, but I had a pretty good rock horse—an old Morgan mare.

I thought if I could get close enough to the goats, I could rope them. We worked at that blamed thing for almost a week.

I hated the idea of goin' over to my neighbor's house and tellin' his wife I lost her goats.

We finally got the silly things down off that mountain. I caught them down in the flats where there is nothin' but mesquite. Peter Moote and I went over and caught one comin' up out of a wash. It was the mother, so we tied her up and let her call her young ones. They get a sense of being wild in just a day or two.

I had a cord, like a window-sash cord, and I made a loop on the end of it. I was goin' to sit down there, feed the animals and rope them. They had been petted and handled before.

I caught one kid.

Jim Hardy, who was almost ninety years old, was there. He said, "Give me that rope." He just threw it over and caught the other one.

Success at last!

To put on that pageant I have no idea how many miles we rode.

* * * *

Then in 1973, quite a while after we had recovered from the goat roundup, they called and asked if I could haul a burro.

I said, "Sure. What's the scoop?"

I was told, "We've got to have somebody haul it from New River Canyon for the pageant."

I went down with a trailer to pick up the burro. I took my young wrangler, Roy Hunt, with me. I said, "They can be stubborn, oh, man. We'll have to pick it up and set it in there." I didn't think I could snake it in there by myself. They're as stubborn as mules.

We got there and opened up the trailer. I was standin' there talkin' to the woman who owned it, and the burro just walked up into the trailer and looked back at me.

I had anticipated loadin' a piece at a time. You can't tell a thing about burros.

Chapter 16

A Washtub Full Of Trouble

Years ago I was breakin' some colts for a fellow on the bottom of the Salt River, about ten miles west of Phoenix, where the Gila and Salt Rivers come together. I'd been ridin' them off and on for several hours. I'd go down every few days and ride first one and then another.

On this one day my brother, Skeet, and my brother-in-law, Ervin Townsend (we called him Ole), came with me. After I got through ridin' we decided to go quail huntin'.

The desert was as wild as thunder in those days—real brushy with lots of foliage. There were a few little rabbit tracks and trails around.

Skeet and Ole started scoutin' around and I went in another direction.

I looked off and saw a big covey of quails goin' off to the north and decided to go over to a clearin' about a hundred feet to my right. I decided to jump over a big bush and run over and get in the clearin', so when they'd flush I'd have a chance to start shootin'.

The bush was about three feet tall, I guess. I jumped over. When I hit the ground it was just like as if there was a great big pig or big dog there on the ground. I jumped right on top of him. I almost sat right down on him.

When I landed, I knew it wasn't a dog, a hog, or a person, because I heard that blamed rattlesnake abuzzin' when I hit him. The only thing that I can figure is that I must have jumped right straight on his head, or else he'd agot me.

I think I broke the state broad-jump record in the next split-second. The sight that I saw when I looked back at the snake is something to remember. It was the biggest rattlesnake that I'd ever seen in my life outside of Balboa Park Zoo in California. I saw some big ones and some dandy ones there.

I'd heard some awful stories about some big snakes, but I never thought I'd see anything like this.

It's a wonder he just didn't throw my feet out from under me. He was all coiled up there as big as a washtub. He was bigger around than the biggest part of my arm, and he was still alive.

Right down at the edge of his coils were my toe-prints. Then there were my toe-prints where I had jumped.

I called Skeet and Ole over. "Want to see something?"

"Yeah. What is it?" Then Skeet looked at me and asked, "Hey, are you sick?"

I said, "No. I'm not sick. I'm very happy."

One of them said, "What are you so serious about?"

I said, "Looky here."

They looked down and saw the snake. Their eyes bugged. "Jimminy Christmas, did he strike you?"

"No. He would have if I hadn't jumped on him."

"What?'

"I did. I jumped right over that bush on top of him. The only way I can figure it is that I must have jumped right on his head."

"You must have. He never pinged you?"

"No."

It was only a mile or so back to Wilson Ranch where I was breakin' those colts. I knew Wilson had some beet-pulp sacks in the tack room. They're two to three times as big as an ordinary gunny sack and they're made of real heavy material. I sent my brother-in-law back to get one of those sacks and some bailin' wire.

He asked what I was goin' to do.

"Well, a friend of mine on East Van Buren in Phoenix has a reptile garden and he always wanted me to bring him a snake." I thought, "Well, there's one I won't have to be embarrassed about bringin' him."

Skeet and I stayed and watched the snake. When Ole got back with the sack and wire I put my shotgun on the snake's head and held him down as best I could, tied the bailin' wire around the small part of his neck right behind his big old head. It was just like havin' a wild dog on a wire. I poked the bailin' wire right straight through the end of the big beet-pulp sack and wired it. I held his head with an extra sack while I took hold of the corner of the sack with my other hand and laid him on the floor of the back seat of my car.

Holy smoke, when your hand would go over the back of the seat where he could see it from the floor it sounded just like dogs were fightin' in there. He'd beat that rag tryin' to strike us.

Ole wouldn't ride with Skeet and me. He rode on the fender all the way to the reptile garden.

When we got there, I held the wire so he couldn't strike and we shook the sack off of him. I wrapped the end of the wire around and around the end of the shotgun barrel so I could always hold him away with the shotgun. You know, he pretty near jerked that shotgun away from me several times.

This guy looked at the snake and said, "Where'd you get him?"

I told him and said, "You've been tellin' me to bring in some rattlesnakes to you because you wanted to buy them."

"Yeah," he said.

"What'll you give me for him?"

He said, "I hope he's not hurt any. I'll give you three dollars for him."

I thought, "Holy smoke, I took all this time and lugged that big outfit, a whole sackful of him, in here and took all those chances for three dollars!"

What I said was, "Is that all?"

"Yeah. You mighta hurt him. He might not live."

"That's all you'll give me for him?"

"Yeah, that's all I can give you."

I took my knife out. I carry one of those big, long six-inch blades on my pocket-knife. I have it on the scabbard of my belt so if I get tangled up in a rope or anything I don't have to dig it out of my pocket when I'm ridin' those broncs and handlin' wild colts. Lots of times you have to cut yourself loose from something to keep from gettin' stomped to death.

I said, "If that's all you want to give me for him, it's a cinch he's not for sale for that. I had too many problems bringin' him in and I wouldn't take those chances for three dollars."

I let the six-inch blade out, held the snake down with my shotgun and run the blade right down between his eyes.

The fellow that owned the reptile garden just raised the dickens.

I took my gun off the snake and turned him loose. He still had about six feet of bailin' wire around his neck, which ran straight through and into the ground. He kept throwin' his head and he threw that knife out. It went straight across Van Buren Street and lit in a box of oranges on a fruit-stand.

That snake was just havin' conniption fits. They grabbed him and put the shotgun on him again and held him down.

I went over to the fruit-stand to get my knife. The guy was mad. "What's the big idea?" He was glassy-eyed.

I told him that I didn't throw the knife.

"Well, how'd it get here?"

"You won't believe this, but I ran it through a snake's head and that snake threw it so blamed hard he threw it across the street."

"Wait a minute."

"Come over with me and let me show you." He came across the street, looked at the snake and said, "Well, I believe it."

The snake was dyin' then.

I took the snake home and skinned it. It was seven feet long and big enough to cover a park bench. I showed it around and everybody wanted to buy it.

I salted it and hung it on the clothesline in the back yard.

The next mornin' it was gone. Somebody wanted it more than I did. And I thought that I had gone to too much trouble for three dollars. I had. That's a poor way to make beans. But to have it stolen was even worse.

Chapter 17

Peculiar Characters

One day a fellow named Harry came to me and said he'd like me to take a couple of his buddies deer huntin'.

He said, 'I've heard so much about Seligman and all those thousands and thousands of sections of land. There's an old Spanish grant where nobody has hunted for a blue moon. I don't know how to get in there."

I knew there was deer there from thunder to breakfast.

We had some peculiar characters with us. We had a fellow that was a guard over in the old country for some family. His family had been guards for several generations. He was supposed to be one of the best shots in the world with a high-powered rifle. I knew him for a long time because he was a guard at the high school. He walked just as straight as if you'd driven a rod right straight down through him. He'd shot rifles in contests all over the world, but he'd never hunted in his blamed life.

An old buddy named Bill went with us. He was a guy that

had diarrhea of the mouth. And sometimes you'd of swore that he had constipation of the brain. That jaw was goin' all the time. We used to call him Loudspeaker. He would just yak, yak, yak, yak, yak. He was a little bit on the portly side. He was too fat to run and he couldn't fight, so everything was pleasant. He was a kick in the pants.

Then there was a fellow that was real quiet. He was a doctor. This doctor had been on as many deer hunts as I had, I suppose, but he never turned a hair in his life. He couldn't hit a bull in the fanny with a scoop-shovel at close range. He'd even laugh at himself.

When he came out to my car he was luggin' somethin'. It looked like he had a box of rocks. I asked, "What are you takin' there?"

He asked, "Can I set these in the trailer?"

"You can if you can pick it up." I walked around and asked, "What is it?"

"Shells."

"Shells?" I always took a handful of shells in my pocket, went out and killed the game I wanted and went home and put the rest of the shells back in the box.

That box was about a foot square. It was bound up with heavy cord. It was a full case of thirty-thirties.

We went into a place where there was a great big downed log. It was a perfect place to set your cups and saucers, cookin' utensils, food and stuff. We didn't want to get too close to the spring because that was where the game watered.

We got a good fire goin'. We had almost a case of eggs there just away from the fire a little ways. There was a gallon coffee pot settin' there. Some of them threw their beddin' on the grass and one or two of them had unrolled theirs.

We had one of those thick jars that people used to make home-brew in. This one was about a two-gallon jar full of apricot jelly.

Everybody was talkin' loud. Loudspeaker had the floor and he was yakin'. He wheezed quite a bit. He got gassed in the First World War, I think. He had a great big old gun. I think it was made in Austria. It looked like it would shoot nine miles. The hole that thing made, why, if you shot in front of a deer, he'd fall in the hole and kill himself. The gun was so big you'd practically have to have a pack-horse to carry it. It had a hexagon barrel. Why in the thunder he wanted to take a thing like that on a huntin' trip where you need something light, I'll never know. He was as proud of that thing as a kid with a new red wagon.

While he was talkin' about what a great hunter he was, I picked up a bucket and went to the spring to get drinkin' water. I was on my way back, about fifty or seventy-five feet from the fire and, off to the north, towards the badlands, was a ridge about a hundred yards away. There was a little cedar tree here and a little pine tree there.

Right against the skyline, walkin' right along there were eleven buck—not a doe in the whole outfit. Eleven big buck. They heard Loudspeaker talkin' and they were all standin' lined up lookin' at us, standin' just as still. It was a sight to see. You wouldn't believe it.

I set my bucket down and said, "Hey, you yahoos, look over to the north."

Loudspeaker said, "What?"

"Look at that. Isn't that a picture for you?"

They looked over there and what happened the next thirty seconds I don't think anybody has the vocabulary to tell. Your tongue would get twisted up and you couldn't make it. That was the darndest sight anybody ever saw.

There was a pause. Everything froze. They were wooden people. Then one of the guys grabbed his rifle, but he forgot to put shells in it. He grabbed a box of shells off his bedroll and stood over the fire shakin' these shells in his hands. Two would go in the fire and three in his hands.

The old guard grabbed his gun. Doc came over and said, "Gimme my gun. That's my gun." He forgot that his was still rolled up in his bedroll. They argued and fought over this loaded gun and BLOOIE, BLOOIE, over them and behind them this one guy's shootin' like crazy and the shells that were shaken in the fire started goin' off.

Somebody ran around behind Doc and yelled, "Your gun is rolled up in your bedroll."

Doc decided that he was right. He started runnin' toward his bedroll, tripped and went over, kickin' the coffee pot over. His right hand went in the jelly and his left hand went into the case of eggs. Now if you think he wasn't a sight to be seen. Wellsir, he just started wipin' the mess on the first thing he could see. He got jelly all over his gun.

Those plague-take-it deer had been shot at four or five times and they never moved. Finally they just started to move, trottin' a little bit, then they'd stop and look.

My goodness, you could take a gun and kill every one of them. You know, the fellows shot and shot and shot and nobody ever touched a hair.

Finally Doc got his gun out of his bedroll and he started shootin'. The deer just looked at him.

I got to laughin'. It sounded like a battle goin' on around me. I bet that old mountain was about ninety percent lead when they got done.

I watched the doctor. He put shells in each hip pocket and was sneakin' through the brush. He went off by himself.

The guard went off the other way. I didn't let the other guys go out. Someone would get themselves killed, so I made Loudspeaker and Harry stay in camp.

We watched Doc. He'd go a little bit and get down on his knee and look, take all the time in the world and BLOOIE! He'd churn it real quick, take all the time in the world again and BLOOIE. He didn't hit anything. He went out of sight, walkin' a hundred yards or so, gettin' down on his knees, shootin' and then advancin' another hundred yards. We'd hear him shootin' off up in the canyon.

Maybe an hour later he come walkin' back. There was still jelly on one hand and egg on the other. Oh, he was a mess.

He said, "Let me tell you something, Hube Yates. It's a law of averages I'm goin' to kill one of those things some day."

Then I knew why he brought all the shells.

The next day I saw him in action again. There wasn't anybody around but us and he couldn't hit nothin'.

This guy from the old country come back all bloody. He was steppin' high and he said, "I got one."

I asked how many points it has.

"I don't know."

I said, "There is some wonderful buck in there. I hope you got one of those big ones."

"Yes. I got the granddaddy of them all."

"How come you didn't bring back the liver? We'd go back up and help you carry the buck in."

He said, "I just cut his throat and walked away."

"You didn't draw him?"

"No."

"Well, can you find him?"

"Sure, I can find him. Come on."

He took us up there to some great big boulders with a lot of oak trees growin' up like onions around them. The deer was layin' next to the boulders. I walked up and looked at it. It was a little bit of a tiny thing. I gutted it out for him, tied the four ankles together and picked it up like a satchel and carried it back. I don't think it weighed more than thirty pounds.

You know, he thought it was the biggest buck he has ever seen in his life. We ate it up in two meals at camp. You couldn't take it anyplace. They didn't care so much in those days. Camp meat was a necessary evil. A game warden would come in camp and help you eat it. They don't any more. They'd throw you in jail and throw the key away now.

I went out that evening. I didn't go very far. I looked up and there stood one of the buck. I floor-boarded him, cut his throat, cleaned him out, turned him belly down over a log to let him drain some, was settin' there lookin' around when Harry came up.

"Who's doin' the shootin' here?" he asked. He saw the buck and his eyes got as big as the dickens. He carried my gun and I carried that deer back to camp. It was only two or three hundred yards back. I hung him up maybe fifty feet from camp.

The guys came in. Nobody noticed the buck. Old Loudspeaker was just awheezin' and athumpin'. They sat around camp and told about the buck that they saw. Doc said, "I don't have any trouble gettin' them to stand still for me, but I can't hit them. I'll get one one of these days." He stuck on that broken record.

Loudspeaker went over to his bedroll to get something and bumped into the buck, pushed it aside and looked at it. I've seen expressions like that in motion pictures, but I never did in actual life. He backed away and looked at it.

"Who killed the buck?"

Everybody looked then. They'd all been in camp for forty-five minutes and they never saw that deer hangin' there until Loudspeaker bumped into it. When they did, they just went around and around. They couldn't see enough of it.

That was a thunder of a huntin' trip. I won't say they all got their deer, but they all brought a buck back in anyhow.

We had every kind of peculiar character in our group. Then, to add insult to injury, they had me.

Chapter 18

Fire-Fightin' Preacher

For years while all this huntin', fire-fightin' and everything was goin' on, I was also a minister—worked five or six days a week for the Fire Department and preached on Sundays. This went on for years and years. Finally, a minister moved out here from Kansas City. He was very active and I could wish off some of the services on him and sit back and listen. Then when I got my ranch I sort of eased out of the preachin', although I'm still an ordained minister and occasionally officiate at weddings. I hate funerals though.

I wasn't a typical minister. I know a lot of ministers who can't jack up a car, or change a tire, or shoe a horse, or pitch hay, or anything else. I think that's for the birds.

I guess it was natural that I got into the ministry since my father was a minister and I was raised in a missionary family. My mother and father told us what was the best thing to do and they proved it every day by example.

Everybody, whether he knows it or not, makes an impression,

either good or bad, upon the people he comes in contact with. Everybody that lives a decent life is quite a little missionary himself.

People say, "He never tried to cram his belief down my throat and I never talked religion with him."

But the first thing you know, people get to wonderin' what church you belong to.

But if my belief doesn't help me by showin' me the better way of life to happiness and contentment, then why in the world do I want to cram it down somebody else's throat? I don't think anybody in jail can promise somebody else liberty.

Chapter 19

Cigarette-Rollin'

In the thirties and forties hundreds of conventions were held at the Adams Hotel in downtown Phoenix.

A lot of the conventioneers got their noses a little wet. After the meetings they would walk around town to see what Phoenix looked like.

I was on duty at the fire station one night and looked up and saw a fellow comin' across the street. He looked at me and kind of braced himself to keep his balance. He had a twinkle in his eye when he said, "Howdy, Mister."

I said, "Howdy yourself."

"I guess til I geh plum sober, I guess I'm doin' all rie."

He had a pretty thick tongue. He was studyin' me.

"Quite a town ya got here."

"Yes, I guess it is."

Then he told me where he was from. We talked for a while. Then he reached in his pocket and pulled out cigarette paper and tobacco. His fingers were all thumbs. He finally creased the cigarette paper. He got the tobacco sack and pulled away at it with his fingers. He just couldn't make his fingers work worth a nickel. He started pourin' the tobacco in the folded paper. Well, he poured a little bit in the paper, some on his thumb, some on his hand, and the rest on the ground. He finally took the cord of the sack and pulled it, got it back in his pocket and started tryin' to roll the cigarette.

My goodness, he pulled it half in two. He threw it down and shook his head.

With a twinkle in his eye he got another paper out, folded it and started all over again. You could see he wasn't goin' to make very many trials at it before he was goin' to run out of tobacco. He poured more on the ground than he did in the paper.

He went through the same rigamaroll, then looked up at me and said, "If you'ze any kine of a fren, exerchise a lil western hosatality, you roll me a cigarette."

I said, "Sure, partner, you betcha."

I took his papers and tobacco, although I had never rolled a cigarette in my life. You can imagine how this would look to him, even as drunk as he was. He stood there and eyed me like I was something out of a story book.

I was tryin' to do my best, but I was makin' a mess.

Finally he got real confidential and said, "Well, I'll be go da hell. I din't know youse drunk too."

Chapter 20

Midwifery

I was the midwife when young Hube was born. He was our second son. The doctor never got there.

I'd delivered lots of them when I was on the First-Aid crew at the Fire Department. I'd deliver them on the schoolhouse lawns, in automobiles, oh, man, I'd delivered babies from thunder to breakfast. Of course, I hadn't delivered as many then as I did afterwards.

When you deliver your own it's a special feelin' inasmuch as the way you care for them.

I was never one to be hysterical. I think that's a breed of people.

I think Mother Nature figured that out a long time ago. It's something we can't even duplicate. We can't improve on it. We're just there to help Mother Nature along. We do what we can to ease it as much as we can for the mother, that's all.

There's just a certain pattern, if it's a normal birth.

Then there are those births that aren't so normal.

When I was a Captain of the rescue squad runnin' out of the No. 1 Fire Station in Phoenix, we got a call, as near as I can remember, about two o'clock in the mornin'.

There was a young woman havin' a baby at a private hospital. It had been a big home at one time, with eight or ten bedrooms. They were havin' trouble savin' the mother's life. She had just given birth and they were having a gosh-awful time. They needed our resuscitator and inhalator. It was one of those E & J resuscitators with a self-contained oxygen breathin' apparatus. A little bit of that would go a long ways when you put the mouthpiece on a person. It would throb and surge. The victim *had* to breathe.

There we firemen were in our boots and our turnouts and suspenders. The front of our pants were pulled over with a flap on a ring so you could just step in the boots and keep walkin' when the bells were ringin'. It was a fast-dress job. On top of that we wore our big coats and aluminum helmets.

I had a crack first-aid crew on my rig. I drilled them and drilled and drilled them.

There were none better.

When we went into the room where the delivery had taken place, the room was just so full of ether it would make you woozy. It was just about to blow up with ether.

I got the machine set up and got it workin' on the patient and everything was under control.

There was nothin' to do but just wait, so I began to look for the bathroom. A nurse told me where it was, so I just walked in. It was a big bathroom like they had in homes years ago.

I nestled down on the throne. Then I noticed about six feet catty-cornered from me was a little black baby in the waste basket. I went over and looked at it. The afterbirth was still with it. I put the toilet-seat down, sat there with the baby over my knees and cleaned its mouth out with gauze and started givin' it artificial respiration. I'd put my fingers around it, raise it up and push down on it with my thumbs. In a few minutes it began to get blotches all over it. The blood was beginnin' to circulate. I discovered that it wasn't a Negro baby after all. It was a white baby—a little girl.

When it started gettin' its natural color back I knew I had it made then. It got to cryin'.

I reached up in the cupboard and got some gauze and tied its cord off in two places.

There I was settin' there on this toilet stool with the lid down, with this little thing in my lap, cleanin' it up, and this nurse, probably the one who had dumped it in the waste basket, came through door.

She stood in the doorway. She was so full of ether that she must have thought she was ridin' the ninth cloud somewhere. She looked at me.

I must have been a sight. With those big boots and coat I must have looked like Man Mountain Dean with this little bit of a button in my lap.

I had found some oil and was workin' away with it. She looked at me, then at the waste basket, then back at the baby. She held the door-jamb up, shook her head and closed her eyes.

I said, "It's quite all right. I give it some artificial respiration, cleaned its mouth and nose, and I'm just givin' it a chance."

They were fightin' so feverishly to save that mother that they thought the baby was dead anyway, so they just put it in the waste-paper basket.

The nurse took the baby then, cut the cord between the two ties I had on there, and took it away just the same as any other baby.

* * * *

I was settin' in the fire station on the front of the hook-and-ladder on a Saturday, as I recall. I was just watchin' the traffic go by and I looked up and saw the cutest little girl in a pink starched dress. She looked like she was about three years old. Here she came bouncin' in there.

I said, "Good mornin', honey. What can I do for you?"

She stood up real straight and said, "I'm lookin' for my godfather."

"Oh, does he work here, or did you just see him come in here?"

"He works here."

I said, "Who is this lucky guy, anyway?"

"Captain Hubert Yates."

"Ooooooooooh," I said, "sit down here, honey and talk to me. What's your name?"

She said it very clear.

I said, "Now, hold everything. Did you say your godfather?"

"Yes, sir."

"Where do you live?"

She said, "I live in Flagstaff, Arizona."

"Flagstaff, Arizona," I repeated. I looked up over the edge of the fire-truck and I saw a car in the first parkin' spot next to the fire-station. The couple in it were smilin' and lookin' at us real close.

I asked, "Would those people happen to be your mother and father over in that car?"

"Yes, sir."

"Let's you and me go over and talk to them. All right?" She got me by the finger and here we went.

The little girl's mother told me who she was. I wouldn't have known this couple from Adam.

I had seen her only once or twice. They had pushed the husband out of the delivery room because he was in the road, so I didn't know him.

The mother said that she had always wanted to go to Phoenix to see me, and she wanted her little girl to see me once anyway.

I shook hands with the girl's father and he said, "That's the way we've got it written up—that you're her godfather."

Chapter 21

Kids And Animals

The older son of mine, Jimmy, would get on his skates and get astraddle of his bulldog. You'd hear the awfullest commotion and he'd be comin' down the sidewalk. You couldn't believe that a dog could run around the block that fast. Jimmy would just be holdin' on to the harness.

I said, "How do you slow him down, son?"

He said, "Just pick him up by his tail and he can't go far on his front feet."

That's the way he put the brake on.

He got so he'd run a rope to his ring harness and he'd get in his wagon. The dog would take him wherever he wanted to go. Jimmy would just head him off. How well that dog was trained.

One time they were comin' around the corner and a neighbor's cat ran across the street and up on the porch. The dog made a square corner and took wagon and all about halfway up the porch steps, and piled it up.

* * * *

I got the kids a horse when they were little fellows. There'd be as many as six kids on that buckskin horse—little kids with their legs stickin' straight out. They'd be from the front end of him to the back end.

To get on him, they'd feed him something on the ground and while he had his head down they'd get on his neck. Then when he'd raise his head, they'd slide down to his back. They'd do this until they got all the kids slid on there.

That horse would pull four or five kids' wagons, one tied to the back of another just like a train. They'd go all over the east part of town. Cars weren't runnin' up and down the street like the dickens then. There were a lot of dirt streets.

Jimmy was a natural as far as balance and riding. He gets that from my dad. His balance was superb.

Young Hube, he couldn't ride a lumber wagon. He finally got to be a strong rider, but he wasn't a natural rider. He had to learn how, but both of the boys got to be top riders.

* * * *

Then when young Hube was a rolly-polly kid of about twelve, he, his buckskin horse, and bulldog must have covered a hundred miles up and down the river and out in the hills. They ended up north of Scottsdale at a fenced-in area for goats.

The old bulldog, Sam, saw those five or six goats and jumped the fence. One of them smacked him in the fanny. He grabbed that goat and turned him every way but wrong-side-out. The goat was raisin' the dickens.

Off of the horse Hube come and crawled through the fence. He went in and grabbed the dog. A billy-goat backed off and hit him in the fanny. He had to turn the dog loose to get the goat off of him.

While he was tryin' to get through the fence, he had to turn the dog loose again and the goat would just knock his block off. The dog would go after the goat and Hube would have to try to get the dog off the goat and make a run for the fence.

The guy who owned the goats come out. He saw a bulldog in the middle of his goat-pen and a kid workin' his goats over. Oh, the guy was ready to kill somebody.

Young Hube said, "I'm tryin' my best to get this dog off. If you'd just hold that goat of yours . . ."

The guy got madder than ever, and every time Hube tried to get through the fence, a goat would hit him in the rear.

He and Sam finally got through, jumped on the horse and rode off. Hube had his hands full though because he had to hold on to the strugglin' dog. Sam wanted to go back and fight the goats.

As the horse carryin' a boy and a fightin' bulldog loped toward Phoenix, the man who owned the goats was wavin' a fist in the air and swearin' vengeance on young Hube.

Chapter 22

The Potato Grenade

During World War II some friends and I went to Nogales, Sonora, Mexico, a few times.

On the Arizona side of the border the Army had set up three tents on the asphalt by the international gate. They had driven great big spikes right into the asphalt to tie the tent ropes to. They had a table, some glasses and a pitcher of water or whatever. Two guards were walkin' back and forth past each other.

People were goin' back and forth across the border. They were allowed to go across and bring back a certain amount of things duty-free. Just as they do today, they had to stop at the inspection station and declare what they had bought. If they were allowed twenty pounds of potatoes and they brought back twenty-two pounds, the border patrol would take the extra two pounds. They got all the potatoes and everything else they wanted.

I reached in the box where they were puttin' the fruit and vegetables and I picked up a little potato, just a nice bakin' size. I had that in my hand and I was just standin' there thinkin' about it and this dad-gummed soldier come by me. I slipped it under my shirt and grabbed my side. He looked at me. I don't know what made me do it, but I said to him, "Do you know anything about these potatoes?"

I jerked the potato out from under my shirt, bit the end off it and threw it—just like a hand-grenade.

He started runnin' and he hit one of those tent ropes and pulled those big spikes right out of the asphalt. The tent collapsed. He was on his hands and knees. He tore the knees out of his pants. He hit that table with all the glasses and pitcher on it and dumped it over. The noise he was makin' wasn't hardly human. He went clear to the rock wall across the street before he looked back. He tore everything to pieces.

There I was standin' with a mouthful of teeth, sayin', "What in the heck did I do?"

He came back and pulled his gun. I thought he was goin' to shoot me, but I was laughin' until I cried. I didn't think there was anything you could say or do that would blow things up that fast.

My friend in the border patrol saw the whole thing. He came and latched on to me and said, "Let's get out of here before he shoots you. Boy, he's scared to death." He took me away like he was arrestin' me.

We went over to the hotel where I was stayin' and the border patrolman said, "For thunder's sakes, Yates, get out of here."

I hadn't done anything but throw a potato.

Chapter 23

A Turtle-Tip

On that same trip to Nogales, the four of us, three men and the wife of one of them, went into a nice place to eat. We ordered antelope. It's legal down there. They were havin' a few rounds of drinks and I didn't want anything to drink so I got up and walked around. It was a big place.

I noticed the guy at the cash register. He was a mass of scars. They were even on his arms. I bet he'd been in a thousand knife fights. Of course, that's a lot of knife fights. He had been cut all to pieces. Oh, he was a salty-lookin' outfit. I made a mental note of this.

I walked around where they were dancin', past the bar and I got back to the kitchen. I was standin' there watchin' the guys work. They had a great big old U. S. Army stove settin' on bricks about six or seven inches tall. The stove must have been about ten feet long. They had these Army pots that must have held fifteen or twenty gallons. There was a guy sittin' on a lettuce crate cuttin' up one thing and another. Another guy was peelin' tomatoes. He'd dip them in hot water and peel them. It was really a workshop.

I looked at them and they saw me, but didn't pay any attention to me.

I saw something move. It was an upside-down turtle that must have weighed two or three hundred pounds. The way they keep them in one place until they get ready to butcher them is to throw them on their backs.

I looked at that old turtle, walked up and bumped him with my boot. He wiggled a little bit. They are slower than a seven year itch. I teeter-tottered him.

Waitresses were runnin' in and gettin' this, that and the other thing.

I looked up on the side of the wall and there was a hay hook. That's what they dumped him over with.

I thought if the workers looked and saw the turtle slowly walking away they'd come unglued.

Nobody was payin' any attention to me at all. I reached up and took the hay hook and rocked him. He was heavy. I tipped him over and what happened the next two or three seconds nobody can tell you. I thought it would crawl slowly and they'd tip him back over. I had no idea he'd go like a streak of lightning.

He saw that stove and tried to get under it. He moved the whole stove and the hot soup. He squared away and went through all those crates with the guys workin' on vegetables. He cleaned them out like dynamite. There was a lot of yellin' and screamin'. He went through there like a dose of salts.

It was my move. I couldn't grab him. I put the hay-hook back and I walked out of there. I went by my friends at the bar and whispered, "When the roof falls in, I'm over at the hotel room—if I make it." They looked up at me. I walked by the scarred cashier and he eyed me. Oh, he was a mean-lookin' cuss.

When I got out on the street I turned a square corner and walked down to the border patrol. I visited him about two seconds and walked right on over to the hotel. I walked real fast, listenin' to the commotion behind me.

When my friends got back to the hotel they said that dadgummed place was like a madhouse. They asked, "What did you do back there?"

Chapter 24

The Old Goat

I'm not the only one who was a prankster. I had a friend, Jimmy, who was awfully rough with his pranks. As long as nobody got killed, it was funny. He would lay awake at night thinkin' of pranks to pull. He was a gagster from the first water. He didn't care how much it cost to put one over on somebody either.

We had a mutual friend, also a prankster, who was the captain of the detectives on the police force.

I was on duty at the Fire Department one night when the police captain came down and pushed the night bell. He said, "I just caught a couple of boys with an old billy-goat. I'm sure they stole it, but they won't say where they got it. We'll have to hold it until we find out. What shall we do with it for a couple of days until we find the owner?"

"Man, don't look at me," I said. "I smelled it when you rang the bell."

You know, goats stand around and wet on their back legs.

They think that's perfume. The stinkier they are, the better they like it.

I said, "Jim is goin' to have open house at his new home in about a week. We can surely keep it a week."

He started laughin'. "You got somethin'. I'll find a place to keep it." He took it and put it in his chicken pen.

Jimmy's party was to start at one o'clock after his bar closed. When I was sure he wasn't home, I pounded on the door and rang the doorbell. A big, young Negro came to the door.

I asked, "Is Jim home?"

He said that he was down at work. I mentioned the party they were goin' to have, and the fellow said, "Yes, they're goin' to have a time. Come in here and look at this."

The bathtub was full of drinks, all buried in ice. The washtub was all full of the ice and drinks. The refrigerator was full. He had every kind of cold meat you could think of.

"They're goin' to throw one. You're goin' to be here tonight, ain't ya?" he asked.

"Oh, I plan on that," I said. "Say, I've never seen this house." I walked around and went into the bedroom and unlatched two screens on the windows.

Later the captain contacted me and asked, "Have you made the connection yet?"

"I sure did."

Around ten o'clock he brought the goat over. We pushed him into the bedroom, locked the windows and went out the door, lockin' it behind us.

We stood outside in the dark and watched the guests arrive. After all that embalmin' fluid they had to drink at the bar and all the drinks that were in the house, they had bottles with them.

Jim's wife went around to show everybody the house. She opened the bedroom door, screamed and came back out. "Jim, there's an old goat in my bedroom."

He asked, "Who is the so-and-so? I don't mind feedin' him and furnishin' him with drinks, but I want him to stay out of your bedroom."

She said, "It's an old goat."

"I don't care who he is. Tell him to get out of there."

We were laughin' our brains out listenin' to this out in the dark.

Finally she got it over to him, Jim went in and saw the goat layin' in the middle of the bed chewin' his cud. He went to the phone and I wish you could have heard the conversation he had with the desk sergeant. We had him all cocked and primed. He asked Jim the wildest questions.

When Jim told him that there was an old goat in his bedroom the sergeant asked, "Who'd you bring out to your house?"

"Oh, the goat was here when we came here," Jim said.

"Is he drunk?"

"It's an old goat."

"Now, wait a minute," the sergeant said. "If you're tryin' to make light of the Phoenix Police Department you'd better get off the perch."

Then the cussin' match started—back and forth. Then the sergeant said, "Now just hold everything. We're goin' to send a patrol car out there. If this is one of your gags, you're in trouble."

In a little while the night captain walked in and said, "Jim, what's the trouble here? The sergeant's all perturbed."

Jim said, "There's a goat in the bedroom."

It started all over again. "Well, who is he?"

"That's what the desk sergeant asked me. It's a goat!"

They went into the bedroom and there was the goat on the bed chewin' his cud. Everything was clean, but it sure smelled. The goat had been in there two or three hours.

"You don't know who did it?" the captain asked.

"I haven't the slightest idea," Jim said. "Everybody was as surprised as I was."

"The only thing I can do is arrest the goat."

"Take him. Get him out of here."

The captain took him away in the patrol car.

Several days later, when Jim had some company visitin' him from Canada I took him some steaks. He suspected that I had killed something out of season. He whispered, "What kind of meat is this?"

"Just call it wild smathern," I whispered and winked.

A few days later he couldn't praise me enough for those steaks. He said, "We've never tasted such steaks in our lives."

The next day we arranged to have a guy named Clem go to Jimmy's bar and tell Jim that he wanted to talk to him. When he got him alone he said, "Did you really eat those steaks that Hube gave you?"

"Yeah. The most delicious stuff I ever tasted."

"I don't mind tellin' you, but I'll deny it in court," Clem whispered.

"What's the matter?"

Clem said, "Well, they butchered an old goat that the Police Department said they got out of your house."

Jim started spittin'.

To the day he died he never knew who pulled that prank. He accused everybody else but us.

Chapter 25

I Missed You Last Year

In the late 1940's I used to take a group of boys from a boys' camp on an annual horseback ride up to Walpi, on the Hopi Indian Reservation in northeastern Arizona. The little settlement chiseled out of a cliff amazed me.

The horses up there on that hill will walk down those little cliffs with those little tiny feet like mountain goats. If they fall, they'll fall for a hundred and fifty or two hundred feet. They're thin horses. They have no width. There's no space between their two front legs, so they almost bump each other. It looked like both front legs came out of the same hole.

My horses couldn't stand on those trails because they'd need three times that much space. Every one of those Indians' horses have manes like some shaggy dog. Their forelocks hang down over their faces and you can't figure out how they can see.

Those Indians go down in the mornin' and walk all over that valley below with a skin and pick up every little stick until they get a bundle. What I don't understand is how they can come back up without that bundle knockin' them off the cliff. Sometimes the bundles are as big as two or three pillows. They utilize every little bit of a stick for cookin' firewood.

And the children—why, a white person would scream bloody murder if they saw one of their little kids goin' down that trail with a steep cliff on one side. You talk about acrobatic and trapeze stuff—it would scare you to death. I've watched their children on the cliff and reminded myself that they've done that all of their lives, generation after generation after generation, and they think nothing of it.

I got acquainted with an Indian there who was about sixty-five years old. He didn't think much of white people standin' around takin' pictures of things that are sacred to the tribe.

He said, "All our lives, from one generation to another, the sacredness of our ceremonies has passed down through us. I know you don't make light of Indian ceremonials. I know this is not a show with you."

The Indians there had been known to smash tourists' cameras against anything that was handy. I saw this happen on several occasions. There's always somebody who wants to chisel, you know. I've seen somebody tryin' to hide a camera and they thought nobody saw them take pictures, and an Indian would go over, grab the camera they were hidin' behind themselves, and bust it all to pieces.

This Indian friend of mine said, "I want you to meet my father."

I said, "I'd like to meet him."

He took me to a rock house right on the cliff. We went in and he introduced me to his father, who was sittin' back in the corner of a dark rock room. He got up off a buckskin chair. When he came over to me and my eyes got used to the dim light, I saw that his eyes were white. He was blind. He shook hands with me. He was about a hundred-and-thirty or a hundred-and-forty years old.

I'd give a nickel if I could remember that man's name. Here's this old man standin' aside of me, and here's his father, and I'm adrinkin' all of this in, and I never made a note. I could kick myself.

The old man remembered the government treaty they made when the whole Indian village was moved out because of a drought. It's a matter of history. It was way back over a hundred years ago. He remembered his mother draggin' him on a skin stretched between two poles, takin' him about forty-five miles to where there was water. They spent the rest of the summer there where they planted enough crops to keep them together before they went back up to the mesa again.

It's odd to find somebody who lives so much longer than all those about him.

The next year I didn't go there. The following year when I took the boys up, the Indian man said, "My father would like to see you."

I said, "Well, I'm very anxious to go see him."

He took me over to the rock house and, by gracious, I walked in that room and I saw that his eyes weren't white. They were not a blue-blue, but a light blue. He had his eyesight back. He got up and walked over and shook hands with me. He still had a lot of fire in him.

As he walked across that room he said, "I missed you last year."

Chapter 26

Play The Game

The 'forties was quite a decade for me. It must have been my practical joke period. It was also the time when I went on a lot of huntin' trips. If anything silly is goin' to happen, it's goin' to happen on a huntin' trip.

This particular time, four of us were headed up from Phoenix to Kaibab Forest for a huntin' spree. Vic and I were in the back of Herb's Buick and John was up front with Herb. Herb had a walkin' cane hangin' on the lap-robe chain in the back of the front seat. When Vic saw it he said, "Who in thunder uses a cane?"

I don't know why I did it, but out of a blue sky I just said, "Shhh. Shhh."

He said, "What's the matter?"

I said, "For thunder's sake, it's a good thing he and John were talkin'. He mighta heard you."

"Why, what's the matter?"

"Jimminy Christmas, don't you know that Herb's only got one leg?"

"No," Vic whispered.

"Why sure, he's got a wooden leg," I said in a hushed tone. "Why do you suppose he retired from some fire department back East?"

"He never heard me, Hube." Vic was still whisperin'.

"He sure didn't. He's awfully touchy about that. He tries his best to keep people from knowin' it. Don't let him know that you know it."

He asked, "Does John know about it?"

I said, "No."

He said, "Well, just as soon as we stop at Prescott to get gas, I'll take John in the boys' room and I'll clue him in."

"I wish you would," I said. "I'll keep Herb outside. He'll look at his car and so on. Tell John to pretend like he doesn't know it at all that Herb's got that wooden leg."

"Okay, okay."

So when we got to Prescott, old Herb got out and raised his hood, checkin' this and that, gettin' gas and all. John was led back into the little boys' room by his sleeve. Old Vic clued him in on the fact that Herb had a wooden leg from his knee down.

I walked up to Herb and said, "Hey, boy, which leg can you limp the best with?"

He asked, "What?"

I repeated, "Which leg can you limp the best with?" I told him about old Vic and the cane.

He laughed and said, "What do you want me to do—carry the joke on?"

"Certainly. He's back in the toilet tellin' John that you've got a wooden leg. That's why you retired from some fire department back East."

He kept laughin' and said, "Yeah, but if they find out they'll knock my block off."

I said, "Never mind. I'll be with you. Just go ahead and play the game."

"Well, let's see, I'd better make it my right leg, hadn't I?"

"Sure. Every once in a while you pretend like you're tryin' to hide it. Just gently limp on it."

"Okay, it's a deal. It's the right leg."

Both the boys came back out, and I knew that John had been told.

When we got to Flagstaff both the boys wanted to drive from there on. "You're bound to be weary," they said, but Herb wouldn't let them drive.

We got in a snowstorm up at the huntin' camp. Herb jumped out of the car, went to grab an armload of wood to take inside, and John ran around and said, "Come on, you've been drivin' all day. I'll get the wood." They took the wood away from him. "You go on in and sit down and rest. You've pounded that old Buick all the way up here."

"Oh, I'm all right," he kept asayin', but he limped on that leg. Pretty soon he grabbed a bucket to go out and get some water and old Vic said, "Come on, fellow, give me that bucket." They wouldn't let him do a bloomin' thing around camp.

Later Vic said, "Dad-gum, he sure is a good sport. He pretends like there's nothin' in the world the matter with him. You can definitely see he's limpin', but he sure hides it good, don't he?"

That evenin' we got by real good. We had a good supper and everybody was in the pink.

The next day there was a slushy snow. It was as wet as it could be. Herb had a pair of boots that went clear up to his knees. Nobody saw him slip his boots off and on.

The next day he had to get out in that slushy snow and walk and walk and walk. Now, I don't care how good your boots are, if you're in a snow a couple or three hours as wet as that snow was, it's gonna soak through. Well, I had just baked some dad-gummed biscuits and I had put a big stick of firewood on the oven door and left it down. You could sit there in front of the stove and put your heels up on that wood and dry your feet.

Herb came in and his feet were cold.

John went over and took a pull of the bottle. I looked up and saw the look on John's face and knew that something terrible had happened. I looked to see what he was lookin' at.

Herb had undone his boots, pulled his old heavy socks off

and put his heels on that chunk of wood in the oven. There were ten pink ones wigglin' around.

John looked at the ten toes wigglin' and followed the legs clear up—both of them. He looked at Herb, followed them back down again, and got a little closer. He looked like he was seein' a ghost. He looked back around and I knew blamed well the roof was goin' to fall in. He said, "Vic, do you see what I see?"

Vic said, "I don't know. What do you see? What was in that bottle that you saw?"

"That ain't what's the matter with me. Look at what I'm lookin' at."

Old Vic looked down and he saw those ten red toes awarmin' up in the oven.

I knew somethin' was gonna happen. I knew that John threw a pretty good right hand. I could see him gettin' ready. He threw one at me and I grabbed him and got him down in that two feet of space between the beds and I held him there, with him tryin' his best to slug me.

He said, "All right, I can't get up. I can't get you up. You let me up from here, but I'll tell you one thing, that guy's goin' to do every bit of work in this camp from today until this week is over."

He did. The boys would sit on the bed. They'd say to Herb, "Hey, boy, bring me a cuppa coffee. Make it a little strong."

He'd jump. He just fell into the spirit of the game. He'd pour their coffee and say, "And how much cream, sir?"

"Just a touch."

"How much sugar?"

"Just a spoonful."

They made him wait on them hand and foot for the rest of the week. They'd clap their hands and snap their fingers. "Would you run out in the snow and get some more wood?" Out he'd go. "Would you get some more water? This water's too warm. Hand me this. Give me my boots. Where's my gun? Would you lay it over a little closer to the bed, please?" They made him work at a dead run all the time.

Herb said to me over his shoulder, "I told you they was goin' to find that out."

"Well, they didn't give you a lickin', did they?"

"No, but that wouldn't have lasted as long as seven days of this slavery."

Chapter 27

The Short-Cut

Another time when the four of us went huntin', we went into camp slidin' and slippin' in two or three inches of snow. It was still comin' down a little bit.

We got in one of those big old Army tents that they had set up with a wooden bottom on it. For the first two feet up it was one-by-twelves. It made a real nice place for a double bed and a stove.

It was still spittin' snow outside.

I decided to pick up my rifle and go talk to the forest ranger. I knew the fellow. Knew him for years and years. I'd been with him a lot of times when somebody got lost in the forest.

Vic said, "I'm goin' with you. If you're goin' out in the snow, I want to go too."

"Oh, you want to walk over there?"

"Yeah, I do."

"All right."

We visited with the ranger for a little while and then me and my old buddy Vic took out. He asked me where I was gonna go. I said, "I'm goin' up on Little Mountain just west of here. I won't be gone too long. I just want to see what's hangin' around up there. Mostly, I just want to hike."

We started off. It was still spittin' snow. There was a switchback on this steep little old mountain. I don't think from the bed of the road to the top of it was more than three hundred feet. It was rugged and covered with little pines and piñon trees, wild rose bushes and everything that grows out there. It was awfully rough. You couldn't climb it, only on this switchback, even on a dry day.

We puffed and puffed and Vic and I made it to the top. He kept lookin' over his shoulder and said, "Don't you think we ought to go back? Don't you think it's snowin' too hard? We ought to get out of here. Can you find your way back?"

I said, "Why, sure. No problem. Let's go up and see what we can see."

He protested.

We got up on this little old mesa where big old pine trees studded it—just made it perfect for shootin'. We walked along for about a half a mile and him protestin' all the time. "We'd better go back. Come on, Hube, it's asnowin' and our tracks are out. How will we know how to get off this mountain?" Yackety-yack-yack.

I kept tellin' him, "Let's go a little farther."

Finally some big old buck got up. He snorted and started

across that mountain and I floor-boarded him. Down he went. I went over and cut his throat and gutted him out.

Vic was protestin' all the time. "Let's hurry. Let's get this thing and get out of here. How are you gonna get him back now?" There were all the odd questions that a beginner will ask.

I cleaned the snow off a log and put the deer belly-down on it. I washed my hands in the snow, picked up my rifle and he said, "Oh, you're not goin' back?"

I said, "No. You can't tell. We might get that other odd one and we'll have one for you too while those guys are sittin' around warmin' their shins at camp."

He protested, but we kept on goin'. It was snowin' a little harder all the time and gettin' deeper. Finally I turned around and said, "Well, I think we ought to go back."

"That's what I think. That's what I've been tryin' to tell you. Let's get off here. You'll probably never find that buck."

We went on back down and I picked the old buck up, brushed the snow off him, skinned out his shins, tied his feet together and put him over my shoulder. I gave Vic my gun to carry. I didn't think we'd have to walk more than half a mile. We walked through that snow, stumblin', slippin' and slidin' and steppin' in things we couldn't see on account of the snow. When I thought I'd gone quite a little ways, I thought I'd just walk over to the ledge and look off the mountain down to the road at the bottom of the canyon. Shoot, I hadn't gone as far as I thought I had. I laid the old buck down and blew a little bit, rested, got my wind back, picked him up and started on. I walked and walked and walked. I said, "We must be almost to that switchback. I'll just take one more look."

I stepped over to take one last look and see how close I was. There was a great big old innocent white mound of snow there, about the size of a big washtub. I stepped over it very gently, still with this old buck on my back. I leaned over and looked. The road was right straight down below us. The innocent white knob was a big old two-hundred-and-fifty or three-hundred-pound boulder just balanced there. As I stepped on it, it went over the cliff, and I went over the cliff with this buck on my back.

You know blamed well you're not dreamin' and you also know that this is your last jump. Boy, you know you're goin' to die. Why I tried to fight those old horns to keep them away from me when I hit, I don't know. It wouldn't make any difference anyway. I blamed sure wasn't goin' to be alive.

All of a sudden ZOOIE!—I hit a ledge. I don't know how far down it was—whether it was twenty or thirty feet, or what, but when I hit I just plowed the snow and the loose rocks and little pine trees and wild rose bushes. I just tore 'em to pieces. I skidded on it for about twenty-five feet and out into space I went again. I was still fightin' that blamed set of horns to keep 'em from goin' through me when I landed at the bottom.

I still worried about that for no reason at all because I knew I was dead anyway. I hit another ledge and did the same thing.

It must have looked like a snowplow in a high wind the way the rocks and sapplings, vines and bushes were just agoin'. They broke my fall, that's for sure.

Off into space I went again. The next one I hit was the same thing. I looked up and was on a long ridge goin' right down to the road. I thought, "Hey, I'm down to the bottom of this thing, and I don't think I've got a broken bone!"

I couldn't believe it. I kept pushin' this old buck's head away from me. I come to a screechin' halt. My fall had pulled my shirt-tail out. Snow, rocks, and bushes had gone right up under my coat and shirt-tail. I tried to raise up, but I couldn't. I looked like the Hunchback of Notre Dame. I was all bent over with about fifty pounds of that junk packed up in my coat and shirt. I jerked my coat off, undid my belt and shook the stuff all out.

I got to thinkin' about Vic. Jiminy whiz! I turned around and cupped my hands to holler for him to stay right where he was and not to move at all. I'd be up to get him within twenty-five or thirty minutes. I looked up in time to see him walk out to that cliff with a gun in each hand—his in one hand and mine in the other—and step off into space.

Well, I didn't want to look but I couldn't take my eyes off of him. I knew dad-gummed well he was dead. He hit the first ledge and the snow banked up on him and the bushes broke his fall. He plowed right through the rocks, snow, wild rose bushes and pines. He must have gone eighteen or twenty feet along the ledge and off into space again, and did the same thing on the next ledge.

He hit in a different place than I did because he wasn't as heavy as I was with that deer on my back.

Off into space he went the third time, tore through all the young stuff that was growin' as thick as the hair on a hog's back. That saved our lives anyway. He crashed through that and I ran up the hill as hard as I could go. I said, "Vic, for thunder's sake, are you hurt?"

I had known him for years and years and I'd never had him mad at me in his life. He laid those guns down in the snow and raised up. He had a lot of snow, rocks and brush up his coat-tail too. He shook it out, brushed himself off and looked at me. Oh, but he was fightin' mad. He said, "No, I'm not hurt, but no thanks to you."

I asked, "What do you mean, no thanks to me?"

He said, "Listen, you big jughead, you're goin' to kill somebody doin' stuff like that."

"What do you mean—kill somebody?"

"Why you couldn't do that very many times and live."

I said, "You mean to tell me that you think that I walked up there and stepped off of that cliff purposely?"

"Oh, I suppose you fell. Yeah, in a pig's valise, you did. I've been around you too blamed much. That's just exactly what you'd do. You weren't goin' to carry that buck any farther in the snow. You went up there and looked over once and didn't like the looks of it so you went and looked over another place and just stepped off."

I said, "Vic, you're a bigger jughead than I thought you were." But you know, I couldn't make him believe any different to save my soul.

When we came into camp one of the guys said, "You got your hands all bloody."

Vic said, "That's just luck that it's from the deer," and he went on inside.

The guys said to me, "What's the matter with him?"

"Well, let me tell you the story now. I'll tell you the truth." I told them. "Nobody could have paid me enough money to do that, and this big outfit, he thinks that I just got tired of carryin' the buck and I just stepped off to shorten the trip back, come off over that mountain from ledge to ledge and lived to tell the story. Now go get his . . ."

"Yes, that's the story," Vic interrupted. "I know exactly what he did. He's goin' to kill somebody puttin' on those dad-gummed shows for 'em, I'll tell you that."

John and Herb winked at me.

To this day, Vic says, "Don't let anybody tell you that he slipped and fell. I was with him. He just stepped off there to save time, distance and carryin' that weight."

Chapter 28

Crashity-Bang-Boom-Bang

There was one little old thicket of oak on my ranch that grew just like onions in an onion patch. It must have been fifty or sixty feet across it. They grew in the middle of a little meadow. It was just like somebody planted them. Some of them were as big around as your arm and some were as big around as your leg. For the most part, they were a little smaller than that. They grew maybe twenty feet in height, at the edge of a little canyon. If anything such as an elk or deer were in that dense thicket, it could just step out if everything was right, and go right down the canyon.

About the last five days of the hunt I rode by there comin' back to the ranch. It was the closest way. The first time I came by there, there was a big old bull elk layin' down in the middle of it. It was a perfect hidin' place. He'd lay there and watch all around him in the clearin' for seventy or eighty yards. He could get away from his enemies. I had a permit to kill him, but I had been so worried about everybody else that I hadn't killed mine.

As I came by he came out of there, CRASHITY-BANG-

BANG. It sounded like he was movin' hell and takin' two loads at a time. He crash-banged with that big old rack. He spooked my colt and he started buckin'. Land o'livin! I couldn't do nothin'. It was such a surprise party. I rode this colt out and by the time he quit buckin' and bawlin', why the elk was long gone. I told him in two or three different ways that I was against him, but the damage was done.

The next day within an hour of the same time I approached that thicket from the other side. I just got up pretty close to it and out of there came the same elk, I guess. You could just see a blur in there. He kept the thicket between me and him. That silly colt broke and bucked all over the place. I'm against that, but it happened.

The same thing happened about four days out of five. I kept thinkin', "I'll ride another horse by here, or this fool will get educated." Well, I never got him. I came on back to camp.

My wife said, "Do you know what? Tomorrow's the last day of elk season and you haven't got one hunter to take out. You made them all happy. They're all gone. Tomorrow, what?"

"Well, I'll saddle up and go get mine."

We were sittin' at the table eatin'. She said, "Do you hear what I hear?"

"Yeah. I think I do." It was a car comin' in. It was an old buddy of mine from down in Phoenix. Jake got out and greeted me.

I said, "What in thunder caused you to come up here the next to the last day of the season? You just joy-ridin'?"

"I come up for an elk."

"Holy smoke, Jake. Tomorrow's the last day."

"I know it, but I was sittin' around the office. The girls came in and said, 'You know this is elk season?' I said, 'Yep, I sure do.' Then they said, 'If we had any men around this office we'd have some kind of a steak fry or barbecue right after elk season's over. I don't know what's the matter with all the men in this office. They're a bunch of pantywaists.' I said, 'If I wasn't working, I'd go get one.' The girls in the office lit on me. 'Oh, sure you would,' they said sarcastically. And I said, 'If I wasn't working tomorrow I'd go right up on the mountain and bring back a bull elk.'

"They all razzed me. Finally the boss came in. He said, 'I understand that if you weren't working tomorrow that it would be no trick at all for you to go up on the mountain and bring back a big bull elk.' I told him, 'That's exactly what I said.' The boss said, 'Well, you don't have to work tomorrow. I'm giving you the day off to bring back an elk.'

"So," Jake said to me, "here I am. I got off a little early and I came up tonight."

"Jimminy Christmas, Jake, if you're lookin' for 'em that hard, that'll be just the one that I won't find. Everybody's gone away from here with a bull and you come in the last night just at sundown and say that you have to have one tomorrow."

He said, "I'm not going to worry about it. You'll get one."

"Well, let me sleep on it and we'll see what the score is."

We put him up and turned in. I got to thinkin' in the night about that little thicket. What I decided to do was to commercialize on that and kill that darned elk.

I had another fellow at the ranch. We called him Bob. He stayed there off and on about two-thirds of the time when he wasn't out in somebody else's camp. There was a little hard-feelin' between him and Jake. One didn't like the way the other one drove a car, didn't like the way he saddled a horse, and one silly thing after another. They fussed and fumed with each other and I was the go-between. It was mostly in fun though.

When Bob saw Jake he said, "What are you doin' here?"

"I come up to get an elk."

"You just got one day left."

"That's right."

I said, "I've got a place where I think I'll take you two guys just about daylight and anchor you down. It's around the other side from where this bull has been jumpin' up. I'll ride through from this side. I can ride over there in forty minutes. If he keeps the thicket between me and him and I can't get a shot at him he'll run straight over to you guys. It's open shootin'."

They thought that was a good idea, so I got 'em up just at daylight and drove way around so as not to molest this thicket in any way. About a hundred and fifty yards beyond the thicket right out in the clear was a little knoll that kept me from seein' the thicket, but it was all clear.

I let them out behind a big log and they could see two hundred yards each way. I drove clear back, put a saddle on my horse (not that colt), and started right straight through the canyon. I come up out of the canyon, and I know it wasn't over seventy yards to the thicket where those boys were nestled down.

I thought that if I don't get him he will run right over top of them. I eased up over the top and I looked at that thicket. It looked like something heavy was in the middle of it. Maybe it was just imagination because I wanted to see something so badly. He's a dead gosling if he's there, I thought. I rode close and got about fifty yards from it. I looked at it and studied it and pulled my little scope out. It looked to me that there was something in the middle of the thicket.

I put my gun down from my shoulder and rode up about fifteen yards farther and CRASHITY-BANG! It even spooked the horse I was on, it made so much noise. Out come the big gentleman. He headed out of there straight for where those guys were sittin'. I watched him go and started ridin' around the little knoll. I heard some loud talkin' and heard BOOM! Look at that! He powder-burned him, I'll bet. BAM! There went another. BOOM! Look at that! WHAM! Jimminy Christmas, it sounded like the battle of the Argonne Forest. What were they tryin' to do? They were standin' there shootin', so I just rode up behind a big pine tree and waited until the shootin' was all over.

When it stopped there was a lot of loud talkin' and such profanity as you ever heard in your whole put-together. They were sure tellin' each other some stories. I rode right up to them.

The sight that I saw was worth the price. Out there on this cold mornin' on the last day of elk season, standin' in grass about knee-deep was Bob with his pants down around his ankles. He'd been runnin' about thirty or forty yards that way. He lost all of his shells, his tobacco, his pipe and his pocket-knife. He'd lost everything, but his gun was in his hand. His legs were blue. He said to the other guy, "Jake, why didn't you shoot him then?"

Jake was laughin' so much he could hardly talk. The tears were runnin' down his chin. Bob was so mad he couldn't see straight. He was so mad he forgot to pull his pants up. He was just standin' there arguin'.

Bob said, "I'll tell you the story. We set there and set there and about that time I said to Jake, 'This is about my time of day. This is my morning's morning.' I leaned my gun up against that log right there and I squatted down there, and old Jake said, 'Bob, are there still wild horses up here?' I said, 'Sure. Quite a few of 'em. Hube breaks one once in while . . . Wait a minute! That's no wild horse runnin'. That's an elk!' Old Jake said, 'It better not be an elk.' He took two big steps away from the log, put his gun to his shoulder and comin' straight at him was the biggest bull elk he ever saw in his life."

Here is old Bob squatted down in the grass about eight or ten feet from his rifle. He hobbled over to grab it and, from this crouched position, looked up and thought the elk was goin' to run him down. He pointed point-blank at the elk right in his face, not over fifteen feet away, and pulled the trigger. If he had killed it, it would have fallen on him and smashed him. Instead, it turned a square corner and went right straight towards Jake. He was so close to him that he couldn't hit him either. Then he turned and stampeded past Bob again. Bob was still shootin'.

They both emptied their magazines at him and Bob ran as fast as he could, hobbled the way he was with his pants down, and emptied his last shot out of his gun. He said, "We never turned a hair. He was too close to us. I thought sure he was goin' to step on us. You just try to shoot one you think is goin' to run you down. See how you miss."

Jake stood there and laughed. He said, "You just wait until I get—ha, ha—tell the boys-ha-ha—won't they get a bang out of this?"

Bob turned around and said, "Laugh? How are they goin' to know? I'll never tell it."

Jake said, "Well, boy, I will. I will. I couldn't keep this one."

Bob said, "Hube, I never felt so let-down in my life. I've never killed an elk. There was one blowed snot on me. Here I am shootin' at him and I can't hit him. He's too close. I looked through that scope and all I could see was elk."

He was shootin' over him about two feet because the scope is up on top of the barrel.

He said, "I never felt so bad in my life since my mother died."

I thought what a fine thing to liken it to.

It was a strange evening back at the ranch. One guy was laughin' until he just got sick. The other guy was so mad he couldn't eat.

Chapter 29

This Is Retirement?

After I retired from the Fire Department in the mid-fifties, Patsy and I kept our house in Phoenix, but spent as much time as we could up at the ranch on the Mogollon Rim. It's Zane Grey Country, and for a hunter, it was paradise.

One cold day, oh, balls of fire, it was cold, Skeet, my kid brother, came to see me while some hunters and I were skinnin' some elk out. He said, "Had a pretty good season, huh?"

"Yes, I did."

He asked me how I would like to manage a ranch.

I said I wouldn't like it.

"You didn't hear what ranch."

"I don't care."

"You don't want to ramrod a ranch?"

"Nope. I want to fish and hunt."

We just kind of passed it off like that. Once more before he left he asked, "You sure you don't want to ramrod a ranch out of Cave Creek?"

I said, "No."

Cave Creek is near Phoenix and it gets hot there in the summertime.

He said, "I told them I couldn't run you off of this mountain with dynamite." That was all that was said about it. He left.

After the huntin' season was over we came down to Phoenix and sold our Christmas trees.

It was a week or two after Christmas and Skeet came over to the house and said, "Say, have you got any wild trips you're goin' to take in the next few weeks?"

"No."

"I want you to do something for me if you will."

"All right. What do you want me to do?"

He said, "Well, I've been shoein' horses for years and years and I want to go to Yucatan for a month or six weeks."

He had a book for his horseshoein' schedule. Every so many weeks he'd go and trim the horses' feet and shoe them. He had some horses of his own too that he wanted somebody to take good care of.

"I don't want some yahoo to ruin those horses' feet while I'm away. You know all those horses we've got out there at Rancho Mañana in Cave Creek?"

"Yeah."

"He's got about fifteen there to be shod. They're horses you helped break and you've shod them a lot of times. Mine are out at a place they call the Sierra Vista Ranch, about four-and-a-half miles out north of Cave Creek. Some doctor and his wife bought it with the idea of retirement."

He gave me three or four that he wanted me to take care of.

I said, "Okay, I'll do it. You just leave your book right there."

I went out to Cave Creek, and it took me three days to shoe the horses at Rancho Mañana. The next day I went out to Sierra Vista Ranch. I jacked up a couple of horses and put shoes on them. I was just finishin' the second one when a car drove in.

I didn't know the Owens from anybody. The woman jumped out and come over and said, "I'm Jean Owen. Are you Hube Yates?"

I said, "Yes. How'd you know?"

"You're Skeet's brother?"

"Yeah."

She looked at her watch and asked, "How long will you be?"

"Oh, ten minutes."

"Well, come up and have lunch with us."

"All right. I will."

A former owner of the ranch, Nancy Blumquist, and guests from Canada were there.

After lunch Jean said, "You still don't want to manage this guest ranch?"

I asked, "What do you mean—still?"

She said, "You turned it down."

I said, "No, you got me mixed with somebody else."

"Don't you have a ranch up on the Rim?" she asked.

"Yes."

"Skeet went up there a couple of months ago and he asked you if you wanted to manage our ranch. When he came back he said you didn't want any part of it."

"Oh, *this* is the ranch? Heck, I didn't know which ranch it was. Sure, he wanted me to manage some ranch and I wouldn't do it."

She said, "We're still looking for somebody. What's the matter with *you* ?"

I said, "I'm just not interested. I don't want to be tied down."

She asked if I was goin' to shoe again tomorrow, and I said I was. "Well, why don't you bring your wife over and let's have some steaks in the garden after you finish shoeing?"

That night I told Patsy about it, and the next day we went out and got acquainted.

Jean's husband, Jack, was back in Milwaukee takin' care of his medical practice.

Patsy and I talked over the proposition and we said *yes* and we said *no*.

I went back and told Jean that I would take it for about six weeks and we'd help screen the people that applied for the job. "Don't get a couple of cowboys like you have out here," I told her. They absolutely didn't know enough to tie a rope around a horse's neck. They didn't know anything about a horse, and one of them admitted it.

We screened one couple after another. There'd be a wonderful woman and her husband would come in and he'd be just gettin' over one. Another time it would be the woman and another time the man. If we could just get some of those couples rearranged, they'd have a good team. We couldn't find a good couple to save our souls, so Patsy and I agreed to stay for a little while longer.

The Owens wanted to close in the summers. Jean said, "You can't get anybody to come out here in the summer."

"Why can't you?"

She had been told that all the guest ranches close in the summer, so I suggested that we write a brochure and give people some activity in the summer.

"You'll never get anything."

I did more business that first summer than they'd ever done in the wintertime. We had all kinds of people come to the ranch on their vacations. There was one man who said his hobby was ridin' horses. I took him out one time on a horse I called *Frijoles*. That's Spanish for *beans*.

"What's the horse's name?" he asked.

"Frijoles," I said.

When he came back from his ride this man thought that Frijoles was the finest horse he'd ever ridden.

The next day I had a cookout or something I had to take care of, so another wrangler took the man out ridin'. Just as they got back I heard the guest say, "What did you say the horse's name is?"

The wrangler answered, "Beans."

"Those are two of the nicest horses I've ever ridden—Beans and Frijoles."

We had lots of interesting experiences on the ranch, but after workin' there for six years, I decided to quit. After all, I had intended to stay for only six weeks.

Jean Owen said, "Hube Yates, the day you quit, I'm going to close the doors."

She did.

But we didn't leave Cave Creek—just moved to a place where we could keep our own horses and open up a ridin' stable.

Chapter 30

Tinkle, Tinkle, Big Old Elk

One day a buddy was visitin' me out at the old Bigler Ranch east of Heber. We were standin' around talkin' about how the elk had been eatin' the corn that we had planted to feed the calves. While we were discussin' the situation, the dog went up in a dense cedar thicket about a hundred yards away from the first row of corn. Pretty soon he came out of there just as hard as he could run. He came over to us and looked back at the thicket and barked and barked. He went back again. Pretty soon we'd hear him barkin' and out of there he came.

Finally this buddy of mine said, "Hube, ride around there and see what in the thunder is botherin' that dog."

So I rode around and come in from behind. I found a great big old elk cow layin' there. When the dog would come up to her and bark, she'd get up and strike at it with her front feet and go back and lay down. Just as soon as she'd lay down that bloomin' dog would come back and she'd get up and run it off.

I told my buddy and he started laughin'. I didn't think it was *that* funny.

He said, "I'll get my horse and then you run her down towards the cornfield." He was just laughin' until he cried.

I run her right out with the dog yappin' behind her. My buddy roped her right at the edge of the cornfield, jerked her down and hog-tied her. He was makin' a miserable job of it because he was laughin' so much.

He said, "Ride up to the ranch-house and get my pickup and come down here."

I drove it right up to the elk. My buddy had hauled a lot of cows in his pickup so he had high sideboards on it. He also had a pulley that he used to pull an old stubborn cow right up into it. So we just snaked that silly elk right up into that pickup and threw a canvas over it. We drove up to the tool shed and he went in and came out with a bell and a good strap.

He measured the strap around the elk's neck and poked the holes with a leather punch, still laughin'. "Get back there and try to keep her covered up if you can," he said.

Here we were, four miles east of Heber, and we drove about twelve miles west of Heber and backed up to a place near an old ranch-house. We pulled the elk with the bell around her neck out of the pickup, untied her and let her go. That old elk got up and started runnin' with that thing jinglin' on her neck. She turned a square corner—just square—and wheeled and come back at us. The bell would still be jinglin'. She'd turn and go the other way. She just turned and ran and turned and ran. She spent several minutes tryin' to outrun that bell right in front of us. She finally went around the point and went off wearin' the bell.

Several months later, elk season came along. I rode by the old ranch-house up at the Ellsworth's place about the second day of the season and heard some loud talkin' comin' out of the house.

Someone called, "Come on in, cowboy, and have a cup of coffee." I joined them.

One of them said, "We know that there's no milk cows or horses here. That's what the Forest Service told us when they sold us these tags. Everything was legal. This guy goes around the point and you should hear his story."

The fellow they were kiddin' hollered at them and cussed them a little bit from the other room.

The first fellow continued his story: "He went out huntin' this mornin'. He was gone about an hour-and-a-half and he come back and was tellin' us all kinds of wild stories. He claims he heard a cowbell." The three of them laughed. "He couldn't believe it, so he thought maybe somebody at this ranch has got an old milk cow. He walked around the point, and walked right up between some rocks and right up to a big cow elk. And he says that elk has got a cowbell on. He couldn't believe it and he let the elk walk off. After he told us that we said there'd be no more whiskey for him. He was so mad he wouldn't eat."

The guy in the other room said, "I *did* see an elk cow with a bell on."

Two days later I came back in and the camp was all in a turmoil. One guy had gone out the next day and had walked up on that elk with a bell. He told the first guy that he heard the bell and followed the sound of it and saw the elk.

"What elk with a bell?" the first guy asked. "I didn't see an elk with a bell. I was just kiddin' you."

"Oh, get off that stuff. You did too. I walked right up on that old elk." They called the other two guys in and told them the story. Somebody said, "Cut him off. No more whiskey for *you* this trip."

The next time I rode over there, the third man had seen the cow elk with the bell. He said, "I heard the bell and I saw the elk."

There was only one guy left who hadn't seen it and hadn't heard the bell. He said, "First, one guy goes and has so much liquor in him that he hears a cowbell and follows it to an elk. Then he comes back to camp and tells the story so good that another guy had to see it. Then finally three of them saw it." He shook his head. "Three to one, but you'll never make me believe it."

I thought the best thing I could do was just to keep my mouth shut, so that's what I did, but I did a lot of smilin'.

Chapter 31

Maybe you CAN Miss It

I had posted NO HUNTING signs at all the main places around the ranch where people might come through a fence or over it, or through a gate. A few years before, some of these city hunters somehow or other went out and shot one of my buckskin horses for an elk. It just so happened that there was a man on it wearin' maroon pants, a red shirt, and a red hat.

But, anyway, he shot my horse out from under this guy, thinkin' that it was an elk. So I posted this place because I've got three or four palomino colts there. I raise my own horses and break 'em myself. About every other one is light-colored. They're black from the knees down, black mane and tail.

Some guys that don't know an elk from a six-ring circus would shoot 'em. There's a whole world to hunt in, without huntin' around my horses and my house.

I'd been out huntin' with a guy. He collected his game and I showed him how to clean it all out, loaded it in his pickup and got him on his way.

I was comin' across my place about a mile from the house when I saw a guy comin' from my place, walkin' through the pines. He was stumblin' along and lookin' back over his shoulder. He had a rifle.

Uh, oh. I was sure he had killed something he shouldn't of. He's killed a cow or a colt. He looked like he was afraid somebody would catch up with him. I thought he'd start runnin' when he saw me, and that I'd have to run him down to see what deviltry he'd been up to. But, thunder, when he saw me he started runnin' to me. He was about fifty-five years old, I guess—all silver around the ears, and gray. He was out of breath when he called, "Hey, do you know where you're at?"

I said, "Well, I've got a pretty good idea. I'm on my ranch. If you're huntin' elk I've got a pretty good idea where you're at. You huntin' elk?"

"Yeah."

"You've got no business here. Where'd you come through the fence anyway?"

"I didn't come through no fence."

I said, "Oh, thunder and blazes, you *had* to come through the fence to get here. You had to go through two or three fences."

"Oh, I didn't go through no fence at all, Mister."

"Well, no matter, but if you're elk huntin', you've got no business here because this place is posted all around it."

"Listen," he said, "I've been lost all day."

I asked, "You're so blamed lost that you don't remember where you crawled through the fence?"

"I didn't come through a fence. I been lost all day. I can't find the camp."

I asked him what his camp looked like.

He said, "Well, we come in through a town by the name of Heber."

"Oh, you did? And then where did you go?"

"We went out a few miles and pulled off in the pine trees."

"Have you got three new Chevrolet pickup trucks?"

"Yeah. Did you see 'em?"

"I sure did. Rode up on 'em. Each one of 'em is a different color—a loud color."

"That's right. How many miles is that from here—fifteen or twenty?"

"No. It's about a mile-and-a-half, or a short two miles."

"Is that all? Mister, I've been walkin' all day, and I've been lost since early mornin'. It's late in the afternoon now. Where is that place from here?"

"Just follow this trail to my fence, go through and just go right up there about three-quarters of a mile and climb out of the canyon on your right. You'll see it on your right. You can't miss it."

He said, "You know, I could find north and south all day, but if I could have found east and west I could have gone straight to camp."

I repeated what he said just to make sure I heard him right. I said, "You're not only lost, you're confused. It's right up there. You can't miss it . . . Say, come to think about it, maybe you *can* miss it. By golly, you just might bypass that camp. Just follow me and I'll take you back."

I took him up there and asked, "That look like your camp?"

"Yeah. Thanks, fellow. You don't know how much I appreciate this. What do I owe you?"

"You don't owe me nothin', but don't let that camp get out of your sight. You walk straight to that campfire."

I went back to the house and told Patsy about the fellow. We had a big laugh.

The next day I came into their camp from the other side. There were four of them around the campfire. They looked up when they saw me comin'. One of them said, "Howdy, cowboy, why don't you get off and rest your saddle a little bit and have a cuppa coffee?"

"Don't mind if I do." While I was drinkin' the coffee I said, "Say, isn't there another fellow in this camp? Or is he lost yet?"

One of them said, "No . . . oh, you know about that, huh?"

I said yes, and told them I'd found him.

A fellow said, "Well, he's in there takin' a nap."

I advised him, "No matter what, don't let him out of the camp." I had just started to tell them about north, south, east and west, when he come stumblin' out of his tent.

"That's the cowboy that found me. That's the fellow right there that brought me home. How are you?"

"You haven't been lost any more, have you?"

"No. Haven't been out of camp."

I asked, "Did you ever find east and west?" The others looked at me. They didn't know what I was talkin' about, so I said, "He told me he could find north and south all day, but he never could find east and west, and, if he had, he would have come right back to camp."

They just roared, and the fellow with the poor sense of direction looked from one to the other, like he thought, "What are you laughin' at? I don't see what's funny." He tried to talk himself into a little laugh, but he never did get the idea.

I guess that happens to a city man who doesn't have to worry about which direction the sun comes up and which way it goes down.

Chapter 32

The Last Deep-Sea-Fishin' Trip

I used to like to go over to the Coast once in a while on a deep-sea-fishin' trip. I like to fish, but I haven't had much time for it lately. When you're married to about thirty-five or forty head of saddle horses, I'll tell you, you don't get much time to pick many daisies, much less go fishin'.

But a while back one of my buddies, Lester, said, "Hube, let's go deep-sea-fishin'."

I asked, "When do you wanna go? Who'll we take with us?"

He suggested Leroy. "He'd rather fish than eat. And let's get Eddie."

We set the date and we all went over to Long Beach in his car. We went down and bought the tickets for the fishin' boat. It was supposed to leave the dock at one-thirty in the mornin'. It had to go out to the bait-grounds and pick up the bait.

What we didn't know was that they had bunks on the boat.

We're desert rats from Arizona and we didn't know nothin' about the blamed thing.

We went to a picture show and then walked the streets—until one o'clock in the mornin'.

The commercial fishin' boat must have been more than a hundred feet long. It was rockin' and blowin'. I thought, "I'm used to automobiles and horses, but this ocean is kind of quarrelsome." That silly thing looked like an egg-shell out in the ocean. It was just divin' and abuckin', and that deck was as slick as any dance floor you've ever been on. And it started from down at the rail where you fish and just slanted up. The little cabin in the middle of it is like a hump on a camel's back. It was just steep enough and slanted enough that you could slide down to the rail around it.

If the thing was wet, I'll bet you'd just go KAPLOOWIE! That boat was doin' some curlimacues that I didn't like to see a boat do.

We had to go quite a ways to where they had the minnows. By the time we got out there that thing had done two or three back-flips and high-dives. It leaned just like a saucer was goin' to turn over. Then the thing would make two or three big, wild lunges and straighten up and go the other way. Man, you had to hang on to something. That was a thunder of a note.

Eddie came around and said, "Hube, where is your satchel?" Each of the fellows had stashed a bottle in it the night before.

I said, "Maybe it's over in the ocean now, the way this blamed boat's aworkin'."

He said, "If I'm goin' to get seasick, I'm goin' to get so plastered that I won't notice it. I want my jug."

He had no sooner got that jug and got a pull off of it than Lester come up and wanted his jug. I said, "Okay, you guys, you all got a jug in there. I'm the only one who's short. Get your jugs and start drinkin'. Don't bother me."

Leroy didn't take one. He was already a yellow-green color. He said, "I've got to get better to die."

I went in the cabin for a cuppa coffee. It looked like a café. There were planks for a table with wells in it for your cups. Otherwise the cups would all slide down to one end. And when this thing did a backflip, why the sugar bowl, salt and pepper shakers, ketchup, coffee cups and everything would slide. They never filled the coffee cups. They were only half full. Drinkin' coffee was like tryin' to do some trapeze work at the same time. Sittin' in there drinkin' the coffee, it looked like everything was goin' to come down on me, but it didn't.

After I drank my coffee, I went out on deck. It was still dark. I saw this little narrow stairway on the hump in the middle of the boat. It looked like it went up twenty-five feet or so. I decided I wasn't doin' any good slidin' around on the deck like a fool, so I thought I'd go up and see what's up there.

I climbed about halfway up and the plague-take-it ocean turned a backflip and went crazy. It dipped and tipped over on the side, and I'm hangin' over the side upside down, almost. Then it righted itself, and I decided to go on to the top of it. When I got there the boat lunged the other way. Holy smoke, I was sorry I was up there. It could have pitched me right off in the sea. Those guys down in the little cabin didn't seem to pay any attention to it. If it was mine, I'd give that thing to the dad-gummed natives. At the top of that thing there was a little platform. I could just barely see a rope that come down from the top of the flagpole. I had a hold of the railin' with one hand, and

I reached up and grabbed that rope with the other, to support myself.

Off to the left two or three feet, it looked like a wall or something. I wasn't sure what it was. I found out in a minute because that boat took a couple of back-flips in a canyon of the ocean. When I grabbed the rope for support I pulled so hard that I broke the flagpole off. It come down on deck with a bang. Then I jerked loose from the hand rail along the stairway. I thought I was goin' to hit the wall. Well, I hit that wall, but it wasn't a wall. It was a curtain in front of a bunk. I went head over heels into this bunk right on top of some woman.

Oh, I tell you, that's when to look nonchalant and smoke a *Muriel.* It was a thunder of a note! The more I tried to get off that woman, the worse shape I was in. I never felt so helpless in my entire life. I felt like I was somethin' spinnin'. The only noise in that clear night was, "GET OFF OF ME. GET OFF OF ME!"

I never said nothin'. I didn't have anything to say. I thought, "If I can just get my hands somewhere where I can push myself off and fall on the deck." I tried to find someplace to push myself off and every place I put my hands was wrong. I'll tell you, I was as busy as I could be.

Old Eddie was about halfway up the stairs and down he went. He heard some woman hollerin', "Get off of me!" He quit the world. He went and slid around the deck for a while.

Just about the time I thought I had got away from the woman—KA-BLOOIE! I was on my head again and right back where I started from. We just weren't synchronized. She'd kick my hands out from under me and down on top of her I'd go. I finally rolled out of that bunk, but not until I did everything backwards that I could think of. I got a hold of that stair railin' and I went down.

Eddie came up to me and said, "Didn't I hear a woman yellin', 'Get off of me?'"

I said, "If you didn't, you're crazy or deaf. She sure yelled."

"What happened?"

I told him and he laughed and laughed. I said, "You wait until it gets daylight. They must be bunked up there."

Eddie agreed. "They must be. I didn't know that. Didn't know there was women on this thing."

We weren't the only party, but we had thought we were.

I said, "When she comes down, I'll show you who it was."

He asked, "Well, how will you know which one it is?"

"Hey, listen, without tryin', I measured her. I can tell you exactly what she looks like—she and Mae West—and I couldn't help it."

When it got daylight we got braced over in the other point of this thing that was rockin' and buckin'. They hollered to have breakfast while they was pullin' in the minnows for the bait. I was standin' there lookin' out the corner of one eye, and here come this gal. She straightened her hair and straightened her blouse. I said, "There she is. That's her."

"How do you know?"

"How do I know? Listen, that stamped itself in my memory for a long time. I'll never forget that. She was fightin' like a tiger. She upset my applecart every time I tried to do somethin'. She was throwin' me around too. So, there she comes."

She was eyein' all the men. She went in and got some coffee.

It turned out she was the only woman on the boat.

We started fishin'. Everybody threw a dollar in the pot for the guy who caught the biggest fish. There were sixty-five of us on board. We were catchin' some big old yellow-tails.

I'd had two cups of coffee and it was about that time of day for me to look for the office. I saw a guy who had come out of the little cabin and I said, "Say, where's the toilet on this outfit?"

He pointed to a wall at the top of this slick deck. "Right over there."

I said, "Wait a minute. What do you mean, right there? You just pointed to a wall. If I didn't need that toilet, I wouldn't ask you."

He repeated himself.

I could see that one little crack was wider than the other. There was a little knob there about the size of the end of your thumb. The board it was on was about two feet wide.

I walked up this slant and reached up and got a hold of the little pearl knob and pulled it. The door opened. I wondered how in the heck I was goin' to get through that little narrow thing. About eight or ten feet back, like down a narrow hall, was this toilet. I thought, "For thunder's sake, what kind of a contraption is this? It's for midgets. How is anybody as wide as I am goin' to get through that door?"

I turned around and backed into it. I squeezed through this narrow room. Then came the problem of how I was goin' to reach the bathroom stationery. I was settin' there, squeezed in, and I got to figurin' how to get the paper. I finally did, and got more than I wanted. I got a big handful all cocked and primed and stood up. I had to stand because I couldn't even bend an elbow in those cramped quarters. I'm standin' up, leanin' over and that dad-gummed ocean hit a canyon again. Out of that blamed toilet I went. My head hit the door, it flew open and right down that slick runway I went, with my pants down around my ankles. My change was goin' all over the deck.

Who did I hit right in the fanny? *Right in the fanny!* I knocked her flat and fell on her. And she started yellin', "GET OFF OF ME!" Same tone of voice.

The fishermen all looked back. They looked at me and wondered where this guy came from with a big handful of paper, his pants down around his ankles, and he had the only woman on the boat down on the deck. They didn't know where I came from. I'm sure they wondered if they had a maniac on deck.

Now, I'll tell you, that's an embarrassin' position. I tried to get off of her and the more she fought, the more we just rolled around together. Finally, I just laid upside down and got my pants up. She gathered herself up. Her fishin' pole was broken and she never said nothin'. She went around to the other side of the boat and she never did come back on that side. I didn't want to see her either.

I picked up all my change and went to fishin'.

To add insult to injury, when the fish were all caught, I won the prize for the biggest fish. I pulled it up and somebody shot it with a shotgun. I won sixty-five dollars.

With that, I tipped my hat to deep-sea fishin'.

Chapter 33

The Thirteenth Trail Ride

Riders get ready to start on 200-mile trail ride from Cave Creek to Heber, Arizona.
(Photo by Hal Moore)

From Thunder to Breakfast | 197

Trail ride in the Mazatzals.
(Photo by Hal Moore)

Every year when the weather gets hot in Cave Creek, we ride our horses up to the ranch in Heber where it's cool. Then in October we ride back.

We started out one year, the thirteenth annual ride, on the 200-mile trail from Heber to Cave Creek with my younger son, Hube, ridin' tail-gunner. I was ridin' point out in front.

We had about fourteen or fifteen people with us. There was a young bronc-twister friend of ours—a good one. He just worried the champions to death when it came to calf-ropin'. He was about the age of young Hube.

We had a girl photographer from the East coast who decided to ride back at the tail-end with young Hube and the bronc-twister. She thought she might see something that she could get a picture of. They pretty near always make something happen. She rode with them for about a half a day. Then she came up with me, thinkin' that she might see more game.

We finally got up on the Mazatzals on a wilderness area switchback. You could look up ahead of you and see it switch back and forth until the trail got up on top of the mountain. You could look up above you and see a string of horses, and look above that and see another string of horses, and look up above that and see another string. It's awfully steep. We had to stop and let the horses puff and rest a bit.

We were about halfway up on that mountain when I looked back over my left leg, way down the canyon, and saw two lines of horses on this crooked trail.

I saw my son comin' up, ridin' right on past everybody else. He cupped his hands and hollered, "Hold up a minute, Dad."

I held up, but all the way up there I heard him laughin' and laughin'. I thought, "What in the thunder is the matter with him?"

He got up to me and started to tell me something. First he asked, "Have you got on a pair of shorts?"

"Well," I said, "that's kind of a personal question. *Certainly,* I've got on a pair of shorts!"

He just laughed and laughed. Then he turned sideways to me and I could see the blood drippin' down out of his saddle.

"What happened to you?" I asked.

He tried to tell me. He was laughin' so blamed much he could hardly get it out.

Finally he told me. He said, "Right after the girl left, I was just ridin' along lookin' way off down at the bottom of the canyon and I saw this little old forked-horned deer standin' there. Everybody passed right by him. He was standin' there by a big old manzanita tree. He thought he was hid."

Young Hube turned around to his partner and asked, "Do you suppose we ought to?"

He looked around and Hube pointed out the buck. "Right there. Do you suppose we should?"

This bronc-twister shook out a look right now. He said, "Definitely."

He dived right off the trail on the side of that old rough mountain and caught that thing right around the neck. A perfect throw even in all that brush. Both of them were runnin' in terrain where nobody has any business ridin' a horse anyway.

The bronc-twister got him up on the edge of the trail and jerked him down. My son came wheelin' and dealin' down there on this big old tall horse and reached down and picked up the deer's back feet. They just stretched him out there on the side of the mountain. They thought they'd get off and play with him a minute, and then turn him loose. This pony that young Hube was ridin' was a fair cow-horse, all right. He'd hold a calf.

Nobody up front knew this was goin' on.

My son got off his horse and he got to thinkin' that we were gettin' too far ahead of him. He got the rope slack and started to turn on the trail to go up to meet the rest of the horses. When he did, this buck got a lot of slack in there and, before you could blink your eyes, he turned around and took one look at my son and made a dive at him.

Just as he did, this bronc-twister saw it and he tried to jerk his horse. He yelled for young Hube to look out. He hit the end of the rope just as that buck hit Hube right smack in the fanny. Man, he clouted him.

His partner jerked him down then.

Young Hube had on a new pair of Levis. The buck took the whole seat out of the Levis and shorts and did a lot of rough diggin' across the cheeks of young Hube's north end. He wasn't hurt seriously. He was just cut and gouged.

He couldn't stand up in the saddle without gettin' pinched for indecent exposure.

He was doin' a little bleedin' when he wanted my shorts. I rode around the next little point and got off to give him my shorts. He put them on to keep him from bein' right out in the open.

When we got into camp that night at Bull Springs, right on top of the Mazatzals, he built him a needle out of a piece of bailin' wire and took a big heavy cord and went to sewin' his pants. It was short on material, but he had to pull the ragged edges together. He made a ridge about the size of a pencil all over his rear end. When he sat down on the thing, he was not only sore, but was sittin' on those blamed big old ridges.

The next day he had to ride clear down off of the Mazatzals to the Verde River where Red Creek dumps in. You had to sit a good seat in order to protect yourself and the horse, but he couldn't. He was tryin' to ride sidesaddle and everything else.

If you wanted to see something real sweet, you should have seen him strip off to go swimmin' in the Verde River that night. It was just like a map of bloody fingers across both of his cheeks when he got his trousers off.

That's what you call ridin' the trail the hard way!

Chapter 34

The Coddled Egg

In 1967 the whole side of a mountain caved away with me and my horse. This was in Cave Creek. Some people hauled me away in an ambulance. I had five broken ribs, a collapsed left lung and some chipped vertebrae. When you break your ribs, you can't cough, laugh, or blow your nose.

After I got to feelin' a little better, I noticed a new nurse at the hospital. She would take everything so seriously that she was all bug-eyed. One day she came in to give me a shot in my hip. Instead of snappin' it, she started pushin' the needle in slowly and it stuck. As she pushed, it buckled. I thought she was goin' to faint. I said, "Young lady, if you'd been sat on as many thousands of miles as that old piece of leather has, you'd be tough too."

She was white around the gills and she nervously flew out of the room for a new needle. When she came back I was still joshin' her. She tried again and it stuck. I said, "Just shove it in." She did and it sounded like a nail goin' through a piece of rubber tire.

The next day or two the doctor said I could have a coddled egg. It's like a soft-boiled egg—real gooey. I cracked it with my knife and was surprised that it wasn't watery. I started peelin' pieces of shell off and took my fork to open the skin and pour it into my saucer, but found that it was as hard-boiled as an Easter egg.

I rang the bell and who should come in but the new nurse, still atwitter over that needle deal. I asked, "You were here when the doctor said I was to have a coddled egg?"

She said, "Yes, sir."

"Does this look soft-boiled to you, honey?"

She looked at it and said, "Oh, my, let me have that." She took it out and in a little while she came back with another egg. She said, "I don't know why the head nurse was mad at *me*. *I* didn't boil it."

"Shove the old gal in here. Let me tell her," I said.

She left and I opened another hard-boiled egg. I had to ring the bell again. I peeled the egg and when she came in I threw it on the floor. It bounced like a golf-ball. She backed away and looked at it and then looked back at me. She finally picked it up and put it on a piece of paper and left.

Then here come two of them. The older woman was kind of persnickity.

I said, "There's no use to give this nurse fits and starts. She ordered a coddled egg. She didn't have anything more to do with it than you did. But maybe you did boil it. You look hard-boiled to me."

She almost threw another egg at me.

I've got a cast-iron constitution. As people come and go, things that turn other people wrong-side out don't have any more effect on me than water on a duck's back.

She stood there with her hands on her hips and watched me crack the next egg. It wasn't hardly in the water long enough to get warm. I opened that egg and, so help me, if I don't live to be a second older, lookin' right at me was *an eye*. The old nurse saw it too and looked like she'd been stabbed with an icicle. The younger one drew her breath in too. The egg had been set on and was just warm.

I said to the contents of the eggshell, "Hello, there. You're not the only one lookin' the detail over. Well, I'll tell you how these things are. If that's the best they can do here . . ." and with that I swallowed the egg embryo.

That caused a little commotion. That nurse wasn't as hard as she thought she was. She almost vomited. She went out of there just aflyin'. Nurses would come by my room and look in at me.

When I could finally get up out of bed I walked miles and miles around that room. The doctor wouldn't come to see me any more because I was wantin' to go home. I was really gripin'. "My wife gives shots better than the nurses do. Any thing you do here that can't be done at home, I'd like to know what it is. I'm goin' home."

On the tenth day the doctor come in and said, "I know I can't hide from you any longer. I guess you want to go home."

I said, "Yes, sir." But what I didn't tell that doctor was that three days later I was goin' on my annual two-hundred-mile trail ride by horseback from Cave Creek to my ranch at Heber.

It just killed me to ride in a car, even for a little while. But on horseback I'd get synchronized with the horse. Oh, you talk about takin' a pain pill, ridin' that horse felt just right. It never hurt me one speck.

It just happened that a photographer by the name of Hal Moore took that trip with us. I had all my riders mounted and we were ready to ride off when Hal said, "Say, I've got one more picture left. Grab your family and go over in front of the tackroom."

We did it just like that. The kids were anxious to go and so were the horses. We just all got in a bunch. It was no rhyme, rhythm, or sense. I looked kind of peaked. I still couldn't saddle a horse, but I could get on one.

Hal brought me that picture afterwards and it looked like the stage had been set for it.

I've had people say, "Whoever set that up and picked those costumes did a good job."

Grandmother's gray geese, that's exactly the way we took off.

Grandchildren Jim, John, Karen Sue and Eddie, son Hube, Patsy, Hube, and son Jim lined up in 1967 for a family photo just before the start of the trail ride.

(Photo by Hal Moore)

Chapter 35

Thoughts on Huntin'

I don't get a chance to go huntin' any more, with twenty eight horses to take care of, but my feelings have never changed: I don't want to kill anything that I can't use.

People come up to me and say, "I've raised that calf so we'd have some good meat, and now we can't eat it."

I'm very glad that I'm not blessed with *that*. I don't like to take life either, but it's the fulfilling of the purpose of life itself. I don't let an animal suffer. It doesn't know when the lights go out.

I have the same feelin' about huntin'. I never like to wound anything. I'd walk my legs off up to my knees to finish killin' an animal that maybe somebody else has wounded, or maybe one that I got a poor slug in. I've walked and walked, day and night, and tracked and tracked, not to let one suffer. I'd put it out of its misery.

I've always been that way and I don't have any twinge of conscience about goin' out and shootin' a deer. He's like every other thing in the world—he has his growin' season and his producin' season and they taper off—and finally wither and pass away. It's the logic of life. When an old buck deer spends a few years of his life doin' what he was created for, I don't kill him for his rack. Boy, I've given racks away. I don't have any hangin' around the house.

One day I saw a guy comin' in to Cave Creek with a deer head on his car. He stopped in front of a bar and people were out lookin' at it. The Game Warden asked him where the body was.

The fellow said, "Oh, I just wanted the rack."

The game warden ordered, "Go back and get the body or I'll give you a ticket." He made him walk his fanny off until he found it.

I have no use for a guy who snuffs a life out—not for any use to humankind at all—but just for the sake of killin'. I don't like to kill anything.

Chapter 36

Skunks and Friends

One summer day about 1968 or '69 I came down from the ranch at Heber for supplies and I came on out to Cave Creek. Of course, I always have some of my friends that I always like to say hello to when I'm there.

I went over to see my old buddy George Councilman. He come walkin' out to me. I thought, "Goodness, gracious, he walks like he's a hundred years old."

I knew he had a bad back a time or two and had to baby it along. This time he had a goodie. He was bent over like he had curvature of the spine. Just the pain on his face hurt me. I said, "George, did you go down to see a chiropractor?"

He said, "No. I'll tell you, it's so sore I couldn't allow anybody to touch it. It'll get better by itself. It always does. I have them every once in a while."

I walked back into his house. He tried to find a chair that he could sit down in. It was absolutely painful to watch him. He was goin' through a lot. You could tell by the way he flinched and gritted his teeth. He finally got down in a chair—sat in it sideways. He said he was goin' to have to put some more hot pads on his back.

I said, "Why don't you go to a chiropractor and get that vertebrae jerked into place?" I tried again to sell him that idea.

I visited with him a couple of hours and the next mornin' I went on back up to the ranch.

I guess I was there a week or so and I had to come down for something. I got my supplies and went to see George. He was just the same as he was when I was there before. He couldn't lay down. He couldn't get in a comfortable place. He had his wife puttin' hot stuff on his back at night until he was almost blistered.

I said, "Doggone it, you know better. Why don't you go down and grit your teeth, or take a shot of somethin' and let a chiropractor straighten that out? I haven't seen you for over a week, and there's no tellin' how long you had it before I saw you. I'm a coward too, but I'd sure get that thing pulled in shape."

He said he'd think about it.

I took care of the business I had come for and went back to Heber.

* * * *

It wasn't any more than ten days later that I was sittin' out in front of the house with a window-sash cord a little smaller around than an average pencil. I was makin' a loop at the end of the cord because a skunk had got down in the basement and was walkin' around between the cases of stuff. We left the door open at night to let it get good and cool, and we'd close it up in the daytime.

If I sat real still he'd come out and walk all around me. He'd eye me and look like he was goin' to plaster me, but he wouldn't.

While I was sittin' there makin' the loop, a truck drove up and stopped in front of the gate. I recognized George's pickup. I thought he was just goin' to sit there, but when I walked out, he was tryin' to get out. His back was just as bad as it was two or three weeks before.

It hurt me to see him get out of that truck. He finally made it and held the truck up for a little bit. I shook hands with him. He looked like he had been run through a knothole. It took him a long time to walk that hundred feet to the house.

Patsy come out and greeted him.

I didn't know what to put him on. He could hardly sit down.

He finally got seated and said, "What are you doin'? It looks like you're makin' a lasso rope out of a big string."

"I am."

He asked, "What for?"

I told him about the skunk down in the basement. "If I sit there for a while he comes out. I'm goin' to rope him, and then I'm goin' to start runnin' and maybe I can get out of the basement before that stinker can get his gears shifted."

"What? You're goin' to rope a skunk with that?"

"I got to get him out of that basement. I can't have him in there. When he comes out, I'll rope him and when I do it'll take four men and a mule to watch me pass by here because I'm goin' to be runnin'."

I sat on some of the cases, had my loop all ready. I looked up and George was leanin' over the cellar watchin' this thing.

He said, "I wouldn't miss this for all the tea in China."

"Say, you'd better be out of my way when I come out of here."

"Don't mind me," he said.

I must have sat there for five or six minutes. "Don't you say a word or move at all because you'll frighten him away again."

The skunk came out, puffed up, looked at me, stomped his feet and threatened me. I just kept watchin' him. I reached out and put the rope on him. I snapped that up on his neck and I started runnin'.

Now I'm not built too much for speed, but I sure went out of that cellar. The skunk braced himself and up those steps he went.

It was a strong window-sash cord. It would have held a horse for a while.

I was runnin'. So was George. He outran me for the first two hundred feet. He went through the front gate like there was nothin' to it. Run, why he went like the driven snow.

I ran and jumped the fence. It's only about four-and-a-half-feet high. I was goin' to pull the skunk over. I pulled and his nose hit the top rail. I pulled him four or five times, and finally he came over. I took the slack up and away I went.

I had my six-shooter. When I got him away from the house I just threw him and I was right there when he hit the ground and I blowed him all to pieces.

Then I got to thinkin'. "That George Councilman! I feel good and he outran me like I was goin' in the other direction."

I went back to him and asked, "What in the thunder did you do? Did you snap your back or something?"

He said, "I don't know, but I couldn't think of but one thing when I looked up and saw you drop that loop on the skunk and start out toward me. I kind of forgot my misery. I didn't know I was such a hundred-yard man."

But, you know, it jerked a kink in him.

He said, "If I'd known you were goin' to do something like that, I'd have been up here three weeks ago."

He needed an incentive, and he had it. I can think about that when I feel bad, and laugh.

* * * *

I know from bein' out with George why he ran so fast. A year or two before that we were up where the Red Creek dumps into the Verde River. We were on a deer hunt.

I always liked to camp there because of the lightnin' bugs. There aren't many in Arizona.

We were all settin' around camp, had a big fire goin' and my two sons, Jim and Hube, one of my son's brother-in-laws, Clarence Wallace, George and I were sittin' there talkin' about what had happened that day.

There were two of us that killed a buck. They were hangin' there in a big sycamore tree. It was a wonderful place to hang them—limbs were just right.

There was a bamboo thicket that campers would throw scraps into. Varmints would get in there. Nobody would want to walk through it because it was dense. It was a perfect place for rattlesnakes.

We were sittin' around spinnin' yarns and drinkin' coffee and laughin' about the things we had done that day. Finally my younger son, Hube, said to me, "Well, you think I should?"

I didn't know what the heck he was talkin' about, just to pop up like that in the middle of a conversation. I said, "Well, I don't know why not. I wouldn't like you if you didn't."

If he was goin' to act smart, why I was too.

He wheeled and pulled that 357-Magnum and BLOOIE!

I knew what he was talkin' about then. A skunk had come right up to camp. I had my side to it and didn't see it.

Did you ever watch it when a skunk throws it? It looks like a blue oily haze—a real thin, fine haze. If that settles down on you, you just as well burn your clothes.

I noticed that the lightnin' bugs didn't blink any more. It was film enough that it sure quieted them down.

We had to move camp. All the food supplies and everything had to be moved back up on the hill—every blamed thing.

When George had his bad back, he remembered that night when young Hube was actin' smart. He was gettin' out of the way fast, bad back or no bad back.

Chapter 37

Pack-Trips and Weddings

I still take three or four groups of Girl Scouts out for four days apiece each summer from their camp, Shadow Rim Ranch, north of Payson.

It started when a couple of big sedans drove up to my ranch some years back. The people were all from Phoenix, and I knew one of the women.

She said, "We've been over to Show Low. We've been to Springerville. We're trying to find somebody who will take some young women out on pack trips. I won't feel bad if you say no. We'll understand."

I said, "Certainly."

They stopped and looked at me. "You will?"

"Sure."

They reminded me again that they were all girls.

I said, "I've never seen one I was afraid of yet."

Boy, they were jubilant. They said, "We knew you did this for the Boy Scouts. We thought maybe you'd do it for the Girl Scouts, too."

I took them out, twenty-four of them, and I'll tell you for sure, that was a group of well-behaved girls. I took out two more bunches that summer.

They invited us over to Shadow Rim Ranch when they broke up that year at the end of summer. They wanted me to say something, so I said, "With all the officials that are here tonight, I want to say this: I've been in this racket a long, long time. I've never had the privilege of ridin' with a nicer group."

They thought I'd do it once and never do it again, but in my seventies I'm still takin' the girls on pack trips.

On one of our Girl Scout trips about 1970, I had two granddaughters along with me. They were tellin' the rest of the girls about the weddings we have in the beautiful countryside.

One of the counselors they called Redwing said, "What's that about a wedding?"

My granddaughter, Cindy, said, "My granddad marries people out here. There is the most beautiful natural cathedral back in those rocks among the flowers."

Four years later, before I left Cave Creek to make my trail-ride to Heber, the Girl Scout counselor phoned me from a college in California someplace. She said, "The only name you know me by is Redwing from Shadow Rim Ranch. I was a counselor."

I remembered her.

She said, "Your granddaughter told me about a wedding you performed out under the pines up on your ranch. My boyfriend and I have been going together for quite a while. Would you marry us?"

I said, "Why, sure."

Then she told me that she had talked to her boyfriend about it and he was jubilant. He worked in Oracle, Arizona. We set the date before we had another Girl Scout ride and I performed the ceremony.

People came from back East to see this, and from California. There must have been forty people there. They came from everywhere.

The flowers, the grass, the green trees and the rugged rocks that have been there for centuries made a perfect settin'. Most any weddin' would have been very impressive under those conditions anyway, but they went overboard over what I had to say too.

I personalize the ceremony. I never could see goin' to a weddin' and seein' the couple stand up before a minister who mumbles away, and repeat after him one phrase after another. They're so excited they don't know what they're sayin'. It's a lot of ritual that don't mean a bloomin' thing—not a thing. I think a weddin' is the most miserable thing in the world to be long. I've gone to so many of them and I just couldn't tolerate 'em. So, I thought, I'll make my own.

I've married many people, but the weddin' of that Girl Scout counselor and her young man really stands out in my mind as a really beautiful one.

Chapter 38

I Alibied

People are always askin' me to give talks.

In 1974, the day before a breakfast ride on Mother's Day, someone said, "Say, would you talk to us tomorrow?"

Oh, man, they think you can just shut it off or turn it on. I've got my head full of horses, saddles and horseshoes, broken cinches and latigo. I made all kinds of alibis.

She said, "Maybe you will when the spirit moves you."

I said, "No," got a cup of coffee and forgot it, but when I got out there I changed my mind. I told them, "I was asked to talk out here this mornin'. I said no. Many years ago, forty or fifty, I don't remember, but it was a long time ago, someone asked me to talk on Mother's Day. I said yes, and I did.

"A year from that date they asked me to talk again on Mother's Day and I did.

"I think the third time my mother was in the audience. I came home and told Patsy that was the last Mother's Day talk. That's all.

"It's too close to my heart-strings some way. There's too much sentiment connected with it, and it's too hard to try to control your feelin's. You stand there and try to grit it out and it's too hard to say the things that you want to say—and not show any emotion at all. It is for me, when I'm speakin' of my mother or the mother of my sons. It's all in the same category. I refused to do it any more.

"I alibied to you last night every way I could. I said I would not do it. I just changed my mind. I will. It's too beautiful a day and the subject is something wonderful. There is no more beautiful subject than that of mother."

So I started off.

Anyway, I got weak in the knees and did another one.

Chapter 39

I Don't Know How To Be Sick

In April or May of 1974 it was pretty blamed hot when I was shoein' horses. I noticed I'd be under a horse for quite a while and then I'd get up right quick and go over to the anvil to shape a shoe and that anvil all of a sudden would flicker like it was doin' a back-flip or somethin', and then it was all over. I thought it was just blood runnin' to my head because I was bent over under the horses. I shod two or three more horses and it kept it up.

I went over to see the doctor. He whistled and said, "You've got high blood pressure. There's nothing to worry about. We can control it, but you've got to do it. You've got to take this medicine."

So I took the medicine and for a while I was pretty honest about it. I took it regularly—pretty-near regularly, anyway.

I made that annual two-hundred-mile pack-trip in June and I felt all right. I didn't take my medicine when I should have. I'd forget where I put it. Then when it came time to pack for the trail-ride back to Cave Creek in October, I packed my medicine, but again I forgot where. So I had ten days more on the way down and I never felt better in my life. In all the years I've been makin' that trail-ride, I've never enjoyed it more than I did in 1974. Every mile was such a joy. I just felt good.

I'd been down in Cave Creek about twelve or fourteen days when I said to my granddaughter, Cindy, "Honey, is that TV doin' back-flips?"

She said, "No. It's all right. Why?"

I said, "I'd better lay down. That thing's goin' every which-way." By the time I stood up, the whole room was doin' the same thing. I couldn't walk. Cindy and Patsy helped me get in bed.

I ended up in the hospital for nine days.

After I had been there five days or so, the doctor said, "I want you to get up every time you feel like you can."

Well, I was about to climb the walls anyway. I staggered a lot, but the doctor said it was the only way I'd get my equilibrium back.

I walked close to the wall the first day or two, holding on to the railin' around the walls. Patsy walked with me a lot. I staggered like a drunken sailor.

There was a girl whose room was down by the emergency door. I had seen her a time or two in her wheelchair and I'd grin at her as I staggered along by the rail.

About the sixth night I decided to walk down the hall while Patsy went to eat. I walked down to the end and was lookin' out the emergency door. The young woman came out of her room in her wheelchair. I said, "It kind of makes you want to get out and breathe some of that fresh air, doesn't it?"

"Oh, yes," she said. "It really does."

We visited and I found her to be a most interesting conversationalist. She had fallen on cobblestones in Spain and hurt her knees, but had kept on walking. She was in the hospital for therapy.

About the time I was ready to go back to my room she said, "There are two chairs just inside that room. Pull one of them up and sit here a while. Don't go away unless you're real tired."

So here she was sittin' in her wheelchair and me in a straight chair right in front of the emergency door. I was wearin' two hospital gowns—one frontwards and the other backwards. That was to keep my back from bein' too naked and cold. I was sittin' sideways, kind of, so I could look outdoors with my left eye and see her too.

From the other end of the hall about a hundred and fifty feet away came a football player. He wasn't wearin' shoulder pads, but he had his jersey on with a number on it. I said, "Well, I guess the game's about to start."

She agreed.

I said, "Boy, what a build that guy's got. Look at that physique. He walks like a panther."

When he got close to us we could see that he had a handful of papers and had a wild look in his eyes. He was kind of dirty. He came right up to us. I thought it was some friend of hers. She spoke to him, but she thought he was a friend of mine.

He said, "I want to get outta here."

I looked at him real close. On the side of his head he had a big old knot with dried blood on it. Boy, he was wild-lookin'.

I said, "If you're hurt, why don't you go back and get patched up?"

Nurses were always comin' and goin' all the time—except at that moment. I looked for one and the hall was empty.

"Did you get hurt playin' football?"

"No," he said, "goofin' off."

He still wanted to leave, but I tried to convince him to stay. "You don't want to go out in that cold, drizzly night. Go back there and let them take care of you and you'll be in good shape by mornin'."

"I'm goin' to go through there," he said.

"No. This is for emergency only," I told him.

He said, "That's all I'm goin' to use it for." He gave the gal in the wheelchair a big push and made a dive for the door. And there I was sittin' in that gown that's open from behind. When he made that big push at me and hit the door, I latched on to him. I scared him. He fought me like a tiger, but I wouldn't turn him loose. I grabbed the handle on the door. He couldn't have gotten out without takin' me and the door. He looked at me like it was the first time he'd ever seen me. The element of surprise just floored him. He thought he could just shove us out of the way and we'd be on the floor callin' for the nurses to pick us up.

He had his hand reachin', tryin' to find some way of gettin' ahold of me. I held on to his right hand and I wouldn't turn him loose.

He must have weighed a hundred and ninety pounds. When I grabbed his hand I just rolled him right over and *ker-plunk*, set him right down. I know I hurt his hand. I said, "Just set it down right there. I want to talk to you."

He said, "I want to get outta here. I can't even afford this."

I finally got one nurse's attention and called her over. The fellow still had a fist full of papers. There he sat. I told the nurse that here was a young fellow that had been hurt. And I said to him, "If I turn you loose, will you go back with her to your room and let them take care of you tonight?"

He said he would.

Later I was talkin' to the nurse about the young man and she asked, "How did you come to get him?"

I said, "Well, that door said *Emergency Only*."

When the doctor heard about it he laughed like the dickens. He said, "I think I'll let you go home day after tomorrow."

I asked, "What about me shoein' horses?"

He said, "You just shoe all the horses you want to, but remember, you're not twenty-seven. You're just about seventy-two."

I've always been rugged, but I guess I'm goin' to have to listen to reason.

Chapter 40

The Fall of '76

We had a wonderful gang of people on our last trail ride down from Heber in October of 1976—people from the East Coast to the West Coast.

The weatherman was on our side. We depended on Indian summer and, I'll tell you, it was most beautiful. The first day out is one to be remembered. You don't have to apologize to anybody for the looks of the country. We have forests and canyons that are beyond description.

It's a thunder of a long ride to Lake One, our first overnight stop. We made it, but the horses were gettin' just a little leg-weary because that's a long haul.

I was on a mare that I'd raised. I'd ridden her thousands of miles.

A girl who has made the trail ride fifteen times with me rode right up aside of me kind of fast and started to say somethin' to me.

She had forgotten that she had thrown her saddlebag over the back of her horse and run the strings through it, but she didn't fasten it. She'd ridden all day like that.

I looked down and saw that thing come off and slide right down and wrap around my horse's leg. My mare thought that the devil had her. When she stepped, that thing went with her.

Oh, boy, she broke in two in the middle, and I didn't know where in the world I was, but I knew I wasn't in the saddle. I was dizzy goin' through the air, and the next thing I remember was hittin' the dirt.

I've been ridin' all these years and it was only about the second time I had been bucked off. I was pretty well bunged up. Luckily, we had a doctor with us. He went over me real good and said I had some busted ribs. He wanted me to take some pain pills.

I said, "No, I want to know how I feel. I'll get 'em later, but I sure don't want any now."

I didn't take any that night, but the next night I did. By that time I *knew* how I felt, and I knew what was busted.

Being a little leery of hospitals, I asked, "I don't have to go down to the hospital at all, do I?"

The doctor said no, I hadn't punctured my lungs.

* * * *

Our campsites were prearranged stops for Patsy to meet us with supper, so I came back to the camp in the pickup truck with her. My son took over as trail boss. I was done ridin' for that trip anyhow.

You don't know there are so many rough spots in the old trails until you try to ride it with broken ribs in a pickup truck. You appreciate the fact that good roads pay off.

I'm glad it was me that got thrown. It could have been somebody else. This is *my* job. There's nobody that's goin' to die off just because I'm laid up for repairs. I told people, "I'm just like death and taxes, so don't worry about me."

Chapter 41

The Strangest Wedding

One day in 1977 I was sittin' around the place when I got a phone call from a friend. He asked if I had time to marry a couple on a certain date.

I looked at my appointment book and said, "Yes, I have. I don't have to travel too far, do I?" My ribs were still mendin' and it hurt to turn the steerin' wheel.

He said it wasn't very far, so I said I would do it.

When the day came, Patsy said she'd go with me and drive the pickup truck to save the wear and tear on these ribs. I thought it was a good idea and said, "I wish you would."

It was chilly when we rode up to a place that looked like a ranch with two or three houses, only it had an office. I thought it was probably a guest ranch.

I went in the office and a fellow was there in old Levis and a shirt. I thought he was dressed kind of casually for a weddin', but we were early and maybe he hadn't had time to get dressed yet.

Patsy and I drove around for about twenty-five minutes until it was time for the ceremony.

People had begun to gather, but they were dressed kind of haphazard. The man from the office came around to Patsy's side of the truck to invite her into the house.

The truck is kind of high and Patsy could see from the chest up that this guy didn't have a shirt on. She thought that was kind of strange that he wasn't ready for the weddin' yet. He was the one who was goin' to give the bride away.

Patsy got out and walked right into him. She caught her breath. He was stark naked. There was no use to turn around and duck and go back.

Oh, dear John, it's hard to say just what her reaction was. Later she told me she thought, "Oh, my soul, we're into this thing and the only thing to do is to do the best you can."

It's hard to describe just exactly what goes through your mind when you discover you're in a nudist colony. It's like, "I don't want to be here, but I'm here. Somebody's got to marry these people."

When we got inside the house I noticed that Patsy looked at the ceiling and the fireplace. She found everything in there to look at but these people.

The bride and groom wanted to be married out in the open. What I should have done was carry the ceremony on and froze them to pieces, but I didn't. They began to shiver a little bit so we went in the house. They told me later that they were glad that I didn't keep them standin' there a long time because they sure were gettin' cold.

They were not good-lookin'. The groom was all hollow-chested, and he was sick. The bride was a poor, thin, skinny little woman.

The ceremony wasn't any different from any other. It's a man and a woman who were goin' to live together, and I think that any promise that they made to each other before their friends and loved ones is important.

I've been a fireman for so long, and I've had to pick up hurt people and people committin' suicide and injured people in every kind of way. I'm not the kind who gets excited about everything. I have quieted down quite a bit over the years. I pretended that the bridal party was fully dressed.

Before we left, the bride took her garter off and threw it. It landed at my feet and I reached down and picked it up. I handed it back to her, but she said to keep it. I stuck it in my pocket, and I still have the silly thing.

I don't know where he got it, but the best man handed me an envelope with money in it. He sure didn't have any pockets.

I was quite anxious to get my wife away because she was embarrassed, so we made our exit as soon as we could. Patsy shook her head all the way home.

I'll tell you one thing, there was never a person who ever lived that looked half as good to me stark naked as they do with clothes on.

A couple of months later while I was loadin' groceries in the truck outside the grocery store, a couple came up to me and said, "Why, hello there."

Of course I spoke to them. So many people have ridden with me that I have to be around them a little bit before I remember their names.

I was very cordial, but after they left, Patsy said, "You don't remember them, do you?"

I said, "No, I sure don't."

She reminded me. "That's the couple you married at the nudist colony."

Holy smoke, I didn't recognize them with their clothes on.

Chapter 42

The Preacher Went A-Huntin'

This huntin' story is the one that got writer Gene Garrison and me started on this book. It took place on the night before the start of the elk-huntin' season along about the end of the 'forties. I had several fellows to take out.

One of the hunters was a great big tall disconnected drink-of-milk from the University of Arizona. He must have been six-foot-six. They sat around the camp there at night and talked a hunt. Slim talked the best hunt there ever was. He'd taken time off from school to come up to kill a bull. Well, he had a gun there that I'd almost be afraid to take out in the brush because, oh, it was just the most beautiful piece of hardware you'd ever want to see. It was polished and in a fur-lined case. It was a beautiful thing. It was old meat in the pot. All he had to do almost was to get the address of the elk and he had his meat. He just absolutely bragged on that gun and his ability.

About daylight we saddled up and the four of them and I went up Black Canyon. It's out south of Heber, and runs through it. We never got out there but about a mile-and-a-half when we saw these elk. There was a whole bunch of them, some of them lyin' down.

Slim shot and blasted the tops off the cedars and scrub oak. He hit everything but the elk. You'd think the way he acted that it was somebody else's fault that he always missed. Before they got through with it there, the other hunters were awfully tired of him.

The day wore on. The other fellows got their elk and hung them up in the pine trees.

The next mornin' Slim and another group of hunters and I got up and went about a mile up the canyon past where we went the day before. These fellows just got off and shot their elk right now. No trouble at all. This Slim just started shootin' the side off the mountain again. He never turned a hair. How many times he shot, I don't know, but he emptied his gun and then he was fit to be tied. He was furious. He acted like somebody had pushed him every time he went to shoot. These fellows couldn't understand him and they were gettin' mad. It looked like somebody was gonna bust him before they got away from there. Anyway, we got these two fellows off with their elk.

I had three more to take out the next mornin'. Slim was still with me. We got up about daylight and I asked the fellows, "Would you like to go out in my pickup? It would save saddlin' up these horses and ridin' up and ridin' back?"

The slim guy said, "Oh boy, I'm for that. I didn't think anything full of hay could be half as hard as a blankety-blank horse."

Well, he couldn't ride, and I had him on a good horse.

Pickups in those days were too small to get too many people in. I put a big four-by-four across the bed of the truck and wrapped some gunny-sacks around it and put one fellow back there, and two in the cab with me.

We had just started to drive out of the gate when a big old black sedan come wheelin' and dealin' up there. You could take one look at that little man and you'd know he was a minister. He didn't have to introduce himself. He wore a little old hat with about an inch brim, like they used back East a lot, and a pair of glasses that he pinched on his nose. There was a little ribbon down to the coat of his blue serge suit, a pretty tie—one of those bow ties that has an elastic band around the neck. His shoes were shined and he had on a white shirt. He looked the part.

I rolled the window down, drove in front of him and said "Good morning."

He said, "Good morning. I'm looking for a Mr. Hube Yates."

"Well, that's me," I said.

"I'm Reverend so-and-so from Cottonwood. I wrote to you some time back about an elk hunt."

"Yes, and I answered you by return mail, and I never heard a thing."

He answered in almost a whisper, "It's my fault, it's my fault. I neglected to acknowledge your letter. Can you still take me on an elk hunt?"

"Yes. I'll tell you what. Just get your suitcase and go out in the bunkhouse, get on your fightin' clothes on, and we'll go."

He reached up and adjusted his glasses. "Oh, I'm ready to go."

The guys in the truck looked at each other. I didn't want to laugh, but it was humorous. "Haven't you got a heavier coat to put on?"

"No," he said. "This is all I have."

Oh, just innocents abroad. The way he talked, it was just something. He was afraid he was goin' to say somethin' wrong, and everything he did say was backwards for a huntin' camp.

"If you haven't got a heavier coat, get your stuff and let's go."

I got one of these fellows that had a heavy coat out of the cab and put him in the back with that slim guy so I could get the minister up front where he wouldn't freeze to death. The canteens on the side of the truck were froze. The horse trough was froze over.

The minister turned the switch, got out of his car and locked it, like somebody was goin' to steal it. He said, "By the way, Mr. Yates, I, uh, I neglected to say . . . do you have a rifle I could use?"

Here's a guy who came elk huntin' with no rifle. The guys in the truck all got real quiet and looked at each other again. They couldn't believe it.

"You haven't got a rifle?"

He said no, so I said, "Oh, yes. I've always got a few of them hangin' on the wall," so I got him a three-ought-six just like they used in the Army. All the little kids that I know can manipulate them. I got two handfuls of shells and come back out and gave them to him and he put them in his coat pocket. It looked like he had a brick in each of his pockets of that blue serge suit. I said, "Here, this shoots just exactly where you put it. You don't have to worry about it shootin' high or low or to one side. Wherever you put that, that's what you're goin' to hit."

He adjusted his glasses and said, "You see, Mr. Yates, I've never fired a rifle."

Great balls of fire! All of these guys looked at me as if to say, "Give him two handfuls of shells and you're goin' to turn him loose on the same mountain with me huntin'? He probably never saw an elk, and he shoots the first thing that moves." Oh, I know what they were thinkin'.

I asked, "You've never fired a rifle?" He said no. I stood there and tried to show him all the points of loadin' and unloadin', the safety and so forth. He talked to himself. He'd have it down on the ground workin' on it. He'd clear his throat and say, "To eject you pull this knob over, and to release it from the chamber you pull it back."

That got a little tiresome, so I said, "Come on, we'll have to go."

The fellows in the truck were gettin' nervous. I took the rifle away from the preacher and laid it in the back. I got him in the truck and we went up the road, stopping before we got to a ridge. I said to him, "Now you can't walk over four miles before you get to the Rim road. If you get that far and you haven't got any game, you build a fire to keep warm. You got any matches?" He didn't, so I gave him some. I said, "Build it in the middle of the road. Sometimes maybe one car will come by a day. Build it in the road. Don't build it in the forest and burn the world up."

He said, "All right."

I said, "If you shoot one, just remember where you shot it, and if you think you haven't gone but a mile, come back here. If you think you've gone two miles or over, go on up to the other road. I'll make this loop and pick you up. It's about thirty-five miles."

He almost whispered, "All right, all right," and he adjusted his pince-nez glasses.

"If you kill an elk," I explained, "you just bleed it." He didn't even have a knife. I told him how to open it up. "We'll be right with you soon if you get something down."

I started to drive off. The other hunters were as solemn as Quakers. The minister called softly, "Oh, Mr. Yates, if I see one, where will I shoot it?"

This brought a grin from all the men. I'm no artist, but I got out of the truck, took a stick and pushed the pine needles out of the way. I tried to draw an elk. I showed him the best places to shoot it.

He looked at me and said, "All right, all right," and he adjusted those blamed glasses.

I got in the truck with the other hunters and started to go around the point about a hundred and fifty feet away where we would be out of sight. We couldn't see him any more, and he couldn't shoot us either with that little mountain in there. I had gone a little way when Slim hollered from the back of the pickup, "Hey, preacher, preacher . . . if you see two, get me one." He laughed.

"All right, all right," the minister said.

I thought, "Well, that's Slim's partin' shot. He had to get his hooks in him."

I drove right around the point and heard a BOOM! I mashed the brakes on. The guy sittin' beside me said, "He killed himself already."

It was too close to where I left him to turn around, so I just shoved it into reverse and backed up. Just then there was another BOOM! The fellow with me said, "No, he just wounded himself first and then he finished it."

Nobody had any idea what in the thunder we were goin' to see when we got around that point.

There was the minister with the gun by the front sight, draggin' it around and lookin' wild. He looked like he had committed the most terrible crime in the history of people. I looked over his shoulder and saw that bull elk just thrashin' and akickin'. Every time the elk would kick, the minister would flinch. Here were these guys sittin' with their mouths full of teeth. I noticed a little fuss over there about sixty yards off to the left. I looked over and saw another elk. Well, for thunder's sake. I never saw anything like it. He'd never had a gun in his hand in his life and he fired two times and got two elk.

The big slim guy was sittin' there lookin' too. I said to him, "You better go over and put your tag on that bull before some ranger comes along and wonders what you're doin' huntin' from a pickup." He looked kind of numb.

I took the gun away from the preacher. He'd pumped it again and was draggin' it around in the brush with it pointed right at his hip. I put it on safety and leaned it up against a tree.

I wiped the frost off a log and took my coat off and laid it down on the log, rolled my sleeves up and went over with a knife and cut this thing's throat. I opened him up. Any hunter'll know what I'm talkin' about. The entrails are held in by their own membrane.

I was reachin' in and rollin' the pouch out. Steam was comin' from the inside of the elk and pourin' by my face. I looked over and saw the minister takin' off his coat, foldin' it up neatly and brushin' off the log to lay the coat on it. He couldn't find a place, so he put it on my coat.

"What are you figurin' on doin'?" I asked.

He said, "Oh, I want to do my part. I want to help."

I said, "I'll tell you what. You just stand back and give me instructions. No use both of us gettin' all bloody, and what the thunder do you want to get that suit and white shirt all bloody for?"

I just dismissed him from my mind for a minute because I was busy. I had split the pelvis bone, and that big manure shoot, oh, it's as big around as your wrist, was coiled up and attached, of course, to the stomach.

Before I could say Jack Robinson, the preacher had reached down into about a hundred and fifty pounds of entrails to help me as I was unrollin' it. He gave it a big yank and it came unglued. It hit him in the face, went around him first and came back. He must have had his mouth open, and the end of the thing hit him in the mouth. It was soft. It looked like alfalfa hay with green paint mixed with it, but it didn't smell like green paint. Well, if he wasn't a sight for sore eyes. One big gob had gone in behind one of the glasses. He was greened out with one eye and he was smeared from thunder to breakfast. You couldn't have taken pains to plaster that on him like that.

There he was, and he said, mumblin' through a mouthful,

"Oh my, oh, dear, oh my." He tried to pull it out the way it went in. He tried to spit too, but he couldn't. He was bridled with that great big manure shoot. I reached up, got it and wound it off of his head. He scooped the manure out of his mouth with his fingers, all the time sayin', "Oh dear, oh dear."

Well, he kept spittin' that stuff up and he gave me his glasses. I pulled his shirt-tail out to wipe them on, and said, "You'll never be able to wear that shirt again. With all that green stuff on it, why it'll always be that way." As soon as I started to hand his cleaned-off glasses to him they would freeze to a light pea-green. I couldn't get it off either. It looked like they had been tinted.

He didn't bother me any more. I went ahead and took care of the elk. When we backed the pickup up to them he didn't even offer to help put it on.

We loaded the two elk and went back to the ranch. My wife had watched me teach him to load and unload the rifle. She shook her head, thinking, "Oh, this is going to be something." We drove in and she came out and saw these two elk steamin', all eight feet in the air. She said, "You got two nice ones." She leaned to me and whispered, "Did you have to kill them?"

I said, "No, the minister here killed them." Her eyes were so blue and glassy. She looked at me as much as to say, "If you don't want to tell me about it, you just keep it to yourself." Patsy was sure I had killed them both.

We took some pine boughs and cleaned some more of the manure off the preacher. Oh, he was a sight. He smelled like it too.

There was a block-and-tackle up in the tree, so I said to him, "I'll pull this elk up in this pine tree here, get the hide off for you, then I'll split it down the middle and it'll freeze good tonight. I'll quarter it and you can pack it in the back of your sedan."

"Oh, no," he said. "I'm ready to go. Can't I haul it just like it is?"

"Why, thunder and blazes, we could put it across the top, but it won't do the top any good."

"I'd like that, if you'd just put it on there. I'm ready to go. You see, they'll be expectin' me back."

I said, *"Who* will be expectin' you back?"

"My little congregation."

"Oh, now, wait a minute. You mean to tell me that you had never hunted in your life, and you told them, 'Well, I've got a permit. I'll run up and I'll be right back. You just wait for me.'"

"Well, yes, kind of like that."

"Well, for thunder's sake," I said. "That's idiotic. Sometimes hunters travel for days and don't get a decent shot. They'll be expectin' you?"

"Yes, they'll be expecting me," he said in his gentle little voice. "You see, Mr. Yates, it's just a little congregation, all working people, and they're poor. They can't afford to buy meat. I told them I'd go up and get an elk and come back and give it to them."

Boy, what a promise! I said, "All right."

I pulled the elk up in the tree and had him back his big sedan under it, then I let the thing belly down on top of it. It sounded like an oil can. BLOOMP-BLOOMP! I tied each of the four legs to the bumpers. I stretched him out and pulled the horns way back and tied them so they wouldn't be bangin' around, cavin' his car in.

All the time the blood was gushin' out, runnin' down in rivulets over his windshield over the sides of his car, freezin' as it went. It piled up about a quarter of an inch before you could flick your eyes. He looked like he was in jail with those blood bars around him. We had to scrape it off with razor blades. If that wasn't a mess. I told him he was goin' to have a problem and that he'd better take the razor blade along with him.

He was ready to go. "Mr. Yates, how much do I owe you?"

"Well, bless your heart," I said, "you don't owe me anything." He knew what he owed me. I gave him the cost when I wrote to him, but I didn't know the peculiarities of the thing then. I wasn't goin' to charge him anything for that. That was quite a show for me.

"Well, I want to pay my way."

I said, "I'm sure you do. Just let these oats be on me. Good luck."

Before he started off I said, "It's a good thing that we got around that point just in time to see you shoot that one and that old Slim here got his gun out and killed that second one because if he hadn't shot that second one, I believe you would have."

He stuttered, "Oh . . . he did . . . I . . . he did?" He knew blamed well he shot them both.

I explained it a little more. "I know that Slim shot that second one because there's a three-hundred-dollar fine and it could be thirty days in jail to shoot two."

"Oh, it is?"

The first thing he'd adone would be to go to his congregation and tell them how he killed the two elk. Why, they'd of had him in the jug. I wished him well and he drove out of there.

This old Slim boy said, "He asked you how much he owed you. You know how much he owed you. He knew it was a hundred dollars, and you told him it was nothin'."

"Oh, I won't worry about that. I'll just put that on your account. He got the elk for you."

Oh, did he blow up. He was teed off then about everything.

I said, "Well, I'll tell you, you stubbed your toe."

Oh, his profanity was enlightenin'. He asked, "What did I do?"

I said, "Here was a man who never had a gun in his hand in his life. I doubt if he's ever seen an elk before. Never fired a rifle. *You're* supposed to be a mighty hunter. You couldn't hit a bull in the fanny with a scoop shovel. You shoot off all the treetops. He comes out and you never ask him what church he belongs to."

"What the hell do I care about what church it is?"

"Well, you should. You should have asked what church he belongs to and join it. You, the mighty hunter, asked him to get you one if he saw two, and he went out there and did it. Shot twice and killed two, and told his congregation he'd be right back. That's a workin' faith and there's some strength to that. You'll *always* be comin' in fifth."

Boy, was he mad!

"Don't feel bad about it," I said. "I stubbed my toe too. When he asked me how much he owed me I should have said, 'You owe me an invitation to come hear you the first time you occupy the pulpit after you get back.' I really would have liked to hear firsthand his interpretation of an elk-hunt."